D0154005

C & C++

Interview Questions
You'll Most Likely Be Asked

326
Interview Questions

VIBRANT
PUBLISHERS

C & C++
Interview Questions
You'll Most Likely Be Asked

ISBN-10: 1-946383-13-9
ISBN-13: 978-1-946383-13-6

Library of Congress Control Number: 2016920130

This publication is designed to provide accurate and authoritative information in regard to the subject matter covered. The author has made every effort in the preparation of this book to ensure the accuracy of the information. However, information in this book is sold without warranty either expressed or implied. The Author or the Publisher will not be liable for any damages caused or alleged to be caused either directly or indirectly by this book.

Vibrant Publishers books are available at special quantity discount for sales promotions, or for use in corporate training programs. For more information please write to **bulkorders@vibrantpublishers.com**

Please email feedback / corrections (technical, grammatical or spelling) to **spellerrors@vibrantpublishers.com**

To access the complete catalogue of Vibrant Publishers, visit **www.vibrantpublishers.com**

Table of Contents

This page is intentionally left blank.

C & C++ Interview

Questions

Review these typical interview questions and think about how you would answer them. Read the answers listed; you will find best possible answers along with strategies and suggestions.

This page is intentionally left blank.

Chapter 1

Memory Allocation

1: Explain the types of memories allocated in C & C++.

Answer:

C & C++ allocates memory as static and dynamic broadly. Static memory is where all the static variables are stored, irrespective of where they are declared within the program. Once the static variables are allocated memory, then the rest of the memory is used for allocating the dynamic variables. Everything other than the static variables is stored in heap and stack. All the variables local to a function are stored in a stack. All the other dynamically allocated variables are stored in a heap. Dynamic memory allocation is unpredictable and it may fail if the system does not have large chunks of free memory as requested. With C's malloc() this is a major issue as for real-time and embedded systems, if malloc() fails it returns NULL which fails the program. In C++, dynamic memory allocation is done using new which is better equipped to allocate memory by reallocating smaller chunks of data as required. Moreover, new does not return a null and instead exits the program. This makes dynamic memory allocation in C++ superior and more reliable.

2: Explain Memory Fragmentation.

Answer:

Memory fragmentation occurs when C's heap does not have contiguous blocks of memory as a single block to be allocated when it is being requested. Consider if your heap has 12K of memory and a 4K is allocated upon the first request with malloc(). Another 2K is requested and that is also allocated, now the heap has a contiguous memory of 6K to be allocated (table 1). If the first 4K memory is freed using the free() and now the heap actually has 10K of memory to be allocated. But it is not contiguous (table 2).

Total 12K of Memory in Heap (Table 1)

4K Allocated	2K Allocated	6K
Req1	Req2	Free

Total 12K of Memory in Heap (Table 2)

4K	2K Allocated	6K
Free	Req2	Free

Now if heap gets a request for 8K of memory, the malloc() will fail even though the heap has free memory, but because it is not contiguous. This cannot be defragmented since during defragmentation, if the 2K lot is moved to the first lot address, the pointer to Req2 will become useless. In Java and other languages that have automatic garbage collection, the issue of fragmentation does not occur as these languages do not support direct access of address through pointers.

3: How is dynamic memory allocation in C different from that in C++?

Answer:

C uses malloc() and free() to allocate and de-allocate memory while C++ uses the new and delete operator to allocate and free memory dynamically. Malloc() is a void function that allocates memory dynamically according to the data type to be created. New is an operator that calls the constructor of the data type or objects to be created and returns the data type created. New never returns NULL. It will throw an exception or terminate the program when it fails. When we call new, the memory is allocated from the free storage whereas malloc() allocates memory from the heap. Malloc() may return NULL when it fails. You have to specify the size to be allocated in bytes when using malloc(). There's an exclusive version of new for dynamically allocating arrays whereas with malloc() you have to calculate the array size and then allocate. The new and delete operators can be overridden whereas malloc() and free() cannot be overridden.

4: Can malloc() fail? How do you handle it?

Answer:

Though it is unlikely that malloc() will fail for a normal program, there is no 100% assurance that malloc() will not fail. For bigger program that request bigger chunks of memory allocation, there is a possibility that malloc() may fail if the system does not have sufficient memory to allocate, is too heavily loaded to allocate memory during the malloc() call or the program is requesting way too large memory than anticipated. Another possible issue is that since malloc() accepts only unsigned int, if you are using pointer arithmetic to find the amount of memory required and get a huge negative figure, malloc() considers it as a positive figure which will be very huge amount of memory to allocate and may fail. Checking for a NULL pointer and exiting the program gracefully one way you can handle the situation. If you do not exit the program and the program aborts, you will have to be prepared for some unwanted surprises. So the best way to handle malloc() is to check for Null pointer and exit the program if malloc() has failed.

5: What is Dynamic Memory Allocation in C and how it is achieved in C Programming?

Answer:

In a C program there are two ways memory can be allocated for the data variables. One of these is to allocate the memory at the runtime, i.e. while the program is in execution mode or when loader and linker finish their task and the program along with all required library functions are residing in the memory. At this stage, memory can be allocated for the program from the 'heap'. This method of allocating memory for data variables during program run time is called Dynamic Memory Allocation. Dynamic Memory Allocation can be achieved by two C library functions 'malloc' and 'calloc' which use Pointer concepts to allocate memory at the run time. The amount of memory required is passed as argument to these functions and the variable for amount of memory to be allocated can be entered by the user while the program is in the middle of its execution; thus achieving runtime memory management in C.

6: What is the difference if dynamic memory is allocated using library functions malloc and calloc?

Answer:

Both the functions allocate memory dynamically, but there is a difference in the way they do it.

Malloc allocates memory in contiguous manner by using the input of how much memory needs to be allocated, then allocates a large chunk of contiguous memory defined in the parameter. Calloc allocates memory that may not be contiguous. It uses two parameters for the number of blocks to be allocated and size of each memory block.

Malloc never initializes its allocated memory , while calloc initializes all the allocated memory blocks to zero.

7: How is run time memory management achieved in C++?

Answer:

There are two operators which perform the task of allocating or releasing memory in C++ run time; "new" and "delete".

While allocating dynamic memory using new, it takes one integer as an argument and returns a pointer of type for which new is allocating memory.

<data type> * new datatype[integer]; Example – char *Ptr_char = new char[10]

In the example, the operation allocates memory for 10 characters or 10 bytes dynamically.

The delete operator takes only the pointer variable that was used while allocating the memory that is going to be released by delete.

delete
<pointervariable_used_while_allocatingMemory_through_new>

8: How is the realloc() function used in C?

Answer:

This function is used to reallocate memory for a predefined memory block to either increase or decrease the already allocated memory. It takes one pointer argument and one integer argument mentioning the new amount of memory block to be allocated. The pointer is the one carrying the starting address of a memory block that was previously allocated. Through realloc(),memory newly assigned may be new memory allocated that is entirely from a different memory place.

<Pointer_Var> = realloc (<Ptr_OldMemoryBlock>, <Int_size>)

Chapter 2

Structure and Union

9: Explain with example how a structure can be passed to a function in C.

Answer:

A structure can be passed by value or by reference to a function in C just like any other data type. The following example will explain how to pass a structure by value to a function.

```
#include <stdio.h>

struct custRecord {
    char *cust_Name;
    int cust_Id;
    char account_Type;
    float acct_Balance;
};
```

```
int main()
{
    struct custRecord addInt(struct custRecord);
    struct custRecord newCustomer = {"Anita", 29017, 'S',
    25892.23};

    printf("\nCustomer Details\n");
    printf("%s, %d, %c, %f", newCustomer.cust_Name,
    newCustomer.cust_Id, newCustomer.account_Type,
    newCustomer.acct_Balance);

    newCustomer = addInt(newCustomer);

    printf("\nNew Customer Details\n");
    printf("%s, %d, %c, %f", newCustomer.cust_Name,
    newCustomer.cust_Id, newCustomer.account_Type,
    newCustomer.acct_Balance);

    return 0;
    }

struct custRecord addInt(cust)
struct custRecord cust; {
    cust.acct_Balance = cust.acct_Balance *110/100;
    return(cust);
}
```

This will output:

Customer Details

Anita, 29017, S, 25892.230469

New Customer Details

Anita, 29017, S, 27186.841797

10: What is the size of the structure address? Explain.

```
struct myAddress {
    char* myName;
    long int myPhNumber;
    char* myStreet;
    char* myTown;
    char myState[2];
    int myZip;
}
```

Answer:

The size of the structure myAddress is 24 instead of 22. This is because when we create a variable of type structure, the size allocated is not actually the total of the size of the member data types. For different machines, the way they allocate memory for certain data types such as int may be allotted memory as much as a character string. Hence, there may be holes in structures generated in such machines and hence, the size may vary. The ideal way to declare a structure to make sure it is allocated an optimum size is to declare the variables in the order of the size required by their data types. Biggest data type variables must be declared first. But this makes the code look clumsy and the programmer may not be able to read it. Since the difference in memory allocated is not too large, for better readability, the data variables are declared as per the functionality.

11: What are Bit Fields?

Answer:

Bit fields in C let the programmer specify the actual data size allowed for the particular member. Even if an unsigned int type is declared, the memory allocated is 4 bytes irrespective of whether or not the data will occupy that much space in memory. Bit fields let you specify the maximum size to be allocated in the memory which optimizes the program. The bit fields also can be used to force alignment of memory allocated. Bit fields cannot be assigned to pointers. It can be used to implement a boundary to the value assigned during the runtime.

12: Write a program to create a dynamic structure array and accept and display the information.

Answer:

```
#include <stdio.h>
#include<stdlib.h>
struct myTrialName {
    int myIntVar;
    char myCharC[30];
};
int main(){
    struct myTrialName *pntrToStrct;
    int counter1,TotalNo;
    printf("Enter TotalNo: ");
    scanf("%d",&TotalNo);
```

/* Allocates the memory for the said number of structures with pointer pntrToStrct pointing to the base address. */

```
pntrToStrct = (struct myTrialName*) malloc( TotalNo *
sizeof(struct myTrialName));

for(counter1 = 0; counter1 < TotalNo; ++counter1){

    printf("Enter the values of string and integer
    respectively:\n");

    scanf("%s%d",&(pntrToStrct + counter1) -> myCharC,
    &(pntrToStrct + counter1) -> myIntVar);

}
printf("For Displaying Information:\n");
for(counter1 = 0; counter1 < TotalNo; ++counter1)

    printf("%s\t%d\t\n",(pntrToStrct + counter1) ->
    myCharC,(pntrToStrct + counter1) -> myIntVar);

    return 0;
}
```

Its output will be

Enter Total No: 3

Enter the values of string and integer respectively:

C & C++

50

Enter the values of string and integer respectively:

J2EE

75

Enter the values of string and integer respectively:

Oracle

30

For Displaying Information:

C & C++   50

| J2EE | 75 |
| Oracle | 30 |

13: How is the memory allocation for a structure different from that of a union?

Answer:

Unions and Structures can be created in a similar manner. They both are derived data types but mainly different in how they are allocated memory space and stored. If you create a union and a structure with the same data types, you will find that a Union will occupy lesser space than a structure. The reason is that for a structure, the size allotted is the sum of the size of all data types inside the structure. But for a union, the size allotted is the size of the largest data type within the union. Consider the following example,

```
struct student {
    char studName[50];
    int class;
    int mark;
}ss;
union student {
    char studName[50];
    int class;
    int mark;
}us;
```

If you check the size of ss and us, you will find that ss will be of size 40 (32+4+4) but us will be of size 32 only. 32 is the size allotted for char array which is the maximum required in the case of the union.

14: What is a Structure in C and how is it different from Array and Union?

Answer:

Structure is a user defined data type which can carry heterogeneous data items like int, char, float, etc. In this way, the data types carried by the structure are entirely defined by the programmer. This differs from an Array that only stores similar data types like either integers, or floating point numbers, or characters.

In Structure, memory allocated for the Structure data type is the summation of memory allocated for all its data members. In a Union the total memory allocated for Union data type is the memory allocated to its largest data member.

15: How to access the members of a structure variable?

Answer:

The members of a structure variable can be accessed using member operator or period operator. A structure variables needs to first be declared, through that variable. The structure members can be accessed using '.' operator.

Syntax:

    <structure_variable_name> .<structure_member>

16: What is the syntax of defining a structure?

Answer:

The syntax for defining a structure is as follows:

```
struct <structure_name>
{
    <datatype> <structure_member1>
    <datatype> <structure_member2>
};
```

17: What is a nested structure?

Answer:

A structure declaration can contain a structure along with other data types, and this is called nesting structures. There are two ways this can be achieved. One is to put the structure declaration inside another structure declaration along with other data types. The second is to first declare the structure that is going to be embedded and then simply declare the already created structure inside the newly created structure along with other data types.

18: Explain the output of the following program.

```
void main () {
    struct A{
        float f;
        int n;
        char ch;
    } A_var;
    union B {
        float f1;
        int n1;
        char ch1;
    } B_Var;
```

> printf("size of structure A is %d\nsize of Union B is %d",
> sizeof(A_var), sizeof(B_var));
>
> }

Answer:

The output will appear as below:

> "size of structure A is 7
>
> size of Union B is 4"

The amount of memory allocated to a structure variable is the sum of the size of all its members. In the above case the size of structure variable 'A_var' is the sum of its data variables f(4 bytes), n(2 bytes), ch(1 bytes), so the total memory allocated is 7 bytes. For unions, the memory allocated is the size of its largest data member. In the above case, memory allocated to union variable 'B_var' is the size of its largest data variable 'f1', which is 4 bytes.

19: Explain the output of the following program.

```
void main () {
    struct student
        {
        int roll_No= 06123;
        char student_name = 'Xyz';
        char section = "A" ;
        };
}
```

Answer:

The above program will give a compilation error since inside a structure or class declaration the variables can't be initialized. Only through structure variables can the members of a structure be initialized.

20: How are pointers to a structure declared? How are members of a structure accessed using this pointer?

Answer:

A pointer of a structure data type can hold the address of a structure variable and then the members of that structure can be accessed using arrow operator. The syntax is shown below:

    <struct_Name> * <ptr_to_structure>;

Example:

    X   S1;
    X   *P1;
    P1 = & S1;

21: What is a self-referential structure? Explain with an example.

Answer:

When a structure carries a pointer member of its own type, then the structure is called a self-referential structure. Generally, this is used while implementing data structures like linked list as in the example below:

    struct Linked_List{
        int D;
        Linked_List * ptr_of_type_Linked_List;
        };

In the above example, the pointer variable 'ptr_of_type_Linked_List' is of type Linked_List.

Chapter 3

Functions or Methods

22: What are the different types of functions based on how they are declared?

Answer:

C language allows the user to create 4 types of functions:

a) Function with arguments and return type. These functions take in the argument data, process them and typically return the result.

Eg: int sum(int a, int b){}

b) Function with no arguments and no return type. These functions are used for general processing. They either access the global or static variables or accept user input once inside the function. They either print the result or assign it to a global or static variable.

Eg: void sum() {}

c) Function with arguments and no return type. These

functions are usually used to print the data passed in a particular format or process and assign to a global or static variable.

Eg: void sum(int a, int b) {}

d) Function with no arguments and return type. These functions access the global or static variables or accept user input to process and return a value.

Eg: int sum() {}

23: Explain the scope rules of functions.

Answer:

The scope rules in any language define the limit or the area that can be accessed by a function or a variable. A function is a named and reusable block of code that serves a particular purpose. The code inside the function cannot be accessed by any other statement outside the function, except for the static variables. If you have a goto or a jump statement inside your program that tries to get inside the function definition, it is a violation of the scope rule of functions. The instructions of a function are hidden from the main program and the only way to access them is by accessing the function. The static and global variables are the only data inside the function that can be accessed outside of it. All other variables are local to the function. C and C++ do not allow functions to be defined inside another function. Every function is an independent piece of code which cannot be accessed by any other entity outside it.

24: Explain the arguments to the main () function in C++.

Answer:

C++ accepts a maximum of 32,767 arguments to the main function. You can pass an int value or a character string to the main program as command line arguments to the program. Command line arguments are the additional information given to a program when you call the program from the command line. The argc int variable holds the number of arguments you are passing to the program and the argv character array holds the array of arguments you are passing to the program. The array's length is not limited since it is given as char *agrv[]. Here, each element in the array is separated by space unlike the other platforms where they are separated by a comma or brackets. Argv[0] will be the program name and then the next element onwards will be the argument passed. For example, if your program name is school and you need to pass the school name and the place it has to be done like this:

school PSBB Chennai

Here argv[0] is school which is the program name, argv[1] is the school name PSBB and argv[2] is the location Chennai. You can pass only character strings to the main and anything else passed will be implicitly converted into a character string.

25: What is a void function in C++?

Answer:

A function is declared as a void function, when it does not return any value to the caller. The function executes normally but does not return any value. If we do not explicitly mention the return type for a function, the compiler assumes it to be an int by default and throws a type mismatch error when the compiler reaches the function call. The function should be declared as void <function_name>(<argument_list>) {}. The function can be called directly as a statement. You no longer need a variable to call a void function. For example,

```
/*Function declaration & definition*/
void sum(int a, int b) {
    printf("\nSum is %d", (a+b));
}


/*Function call*/
void main() {
    int a = 10;
    int b = 20;
    sum(a,b);
}
```

This will give the output as:

Sum is 30

26: What is function overloading in C++ and how does it differ from function overriding?

Answer:

When more than one function in a module has the same name but they differ in their signature, then it is called function overloading. The Signature of a function includes type of arguments passed to a function as well as number of arguments passed. In C++, return type of a function can't be considered as a way to implement function overloading in a program, but in C it is possible. Function overriding is seen in inheritance, when two classes are defined and one is inherited from the other and both carry the same function name including same signature and return type. The logic implemented inside those functions may vary, though it is not mandatory.

27: What is a default argument while declaring a function or calling a function?

Answer:

It is not always mandatory to pass all the arguments to a function while calling it. Certain parameters which can be left out, and those arguments carry default values and hence are called default statements. The default values are provided by compiler while calling the function. The default values are mentioned in the function prototype. But if arguments are passed while calling a function, then they always override the default values defined in the function prototype.

28: Why are functions used?

Answer:

Being able to reuse existing code is the main reason for using functions in a program. They also simplify maintenance and reduce the chance of errors. If a function is called several times in a program instead of the same code appearing in several places, it is faster and easier to create the program and support it, since if a change is needed it can be changed in one place instead of several, which also reduces the chances of errors.

29: What is main() function in C and the syntax of the main function?

Answer:

The main() function is the starting point of the program execution. Program execution begins with the first statement defined inside main() function.

The main() function can't be overloaded.

Syntax of the main function is:

<return type> main ([int x, char *y[], [char **z]])

where x is number of arguments being passed, y is an array of pointers to the command line arguments, z is a pointer to pointer data type and it points to env variables

30: What is the difference the way function prototypes are declared in C and C++?

Answer:

In C, it is not mandatory to have the function prototype before making a call to the function (which is not defined before the call to the function). But in C++, it is compulsory to declare the prototype if the function definition is not yet seen while making call to the function. A function prototype is also mandatory for those functions defined after main() function.

31: What is the difference between parameters passed by value and by pointers?

Answer:

When parameters are passed by value to the called function, then arguments being passed from the caller and being declared in the called function are of same data type. In the case of parameters passed by pointers, the argument being passed from the called function is the address of a variable (not the variable itself), and the other argument is a pointer which stores the address being passed from the caller.

For parameters passed by pointers, any modification to the memory location indicated by the pointer directly changes the variable value whose address is passed as an argument. With values being passed as parameters, the changes are not directly seen in the called function.

32: What is a function and how does it help programmers in developing programs?

Answer:

Functions are like a bunch of codes grouped together to achieve a particular goal. Once a function is defined, it can be called later instead have to write the same code again inside the program. Using functions helps programmers make code reusable.

33: How to call a function defined in a module?

Answer:

A function is called using the function name and by placing arguments required by the function. Depending upon the return value of the function, the function call can also be placed at the right side of assignment operator. The syntax is given below:

<function_name> (<argument1, <argument2 , . . >>); # if function doesn't have a return value

<variable> = <function_name> (<argument1, <argument2 , . . >>); #if function returns some value

34: What is the difference between actual and formal parameters?

Answer:

Actual parameters refer to the arguments present in the argument list of the calling function. Formal parameters are the arguments present in the argument list of called function.

35: What is static binding and dynamic binding?

Answer:

Static binding is a mechanism where It is known to the compiler which functions to be called before the program execution. For example, in operator overloading, It is known to the compiler which function to call basing upon the function signature.

Dynamic binding is the opposite to static binding. Here, the compiler is unaware of which function to be called, so the function which to be called is decided at run time. For example, the call to virtual functions is resolved at run time rather than compile time.

36: How to return a value from a function?

Answer:

To return a value from a function, the return data type needs to be mentioned while defining the program as well as in the prototype declaration if needed. Then in the function definition, the keyword 'return' can be used to return a value of a predefined data type to the calling function. The syntax of return statement is given below:

```
return<expression> ;
return(<expression>);
```

37: What are library functions in C?

Answer:

Library functions are predefined functions provided to programmers to use them inside a program to carry common fundamental activities, like printing a value to the standard output or accepting a value from a standard input. Like a prototype declaration is done for a user defined function, for library functions this is done through header files (i.e. by including header files for each library function before using them in the program).

38: What is a user defined function?

Answer:

Unlike library functions, these functions are defined by the programmer. User defined functions can use library functions inside their body. For a user defined function, It is required to include the prototype declaration before calling them.

39: What is the syntax of a function definition?

Answer:

The syntax of a function definition is shown below:

```
<return type>  <function_name> (<parameter1,<parameter2, . . >>)
    {
    <function_body_multiple_statements>
    return <expression>; # if the function returns any value
    }
```

40: Explain the output of the below program.

```
void func (int ABC[], int N) {
    ABC[N-1] = 60;
        }
void main (){
    int XYZ[] = {10, 20, 30} , i;
    func (XYZ, 3) ;
    for (i=0 ; i<3 ; i++)
        printf(«%d «, XYZ[i] ) ;
        }
```

Answer:

The output will be 10 20 60 not 10 20 30. When an array is passed to a function, then its starting address actually gets passed as the parameter, hence any change to the array in the function to which the array is passed will be reflected in the array for function from where the call was made.

41: What is the difference between pass by reference and pass by pointer while calling a function?

Answer:

In both cases, the address of the argument variables are passed to the function, but in case of 'pass by reference', the addresses are passed implicitly, and in the other case, addresses are passed explicitly through pointer variables.

Chapter 4

Recursion

42: Write a program to print the Fibonacci series using recursive function.

Answer:

The program prints the first 15 numbers in the Fibonacci series.

```c
#include <stdio.h>
int fnFibonacci(int num) {
    if(num == 0) return 0;
    if(num == 1) return 1;
    return fnFibonacci(num-1) + fnFibonacci(num-2);
}

int  main() {
    for (int num = 0; num < 15; num++) {
        printf("%d\n", fnFibonacci(num));
    }
```

```
        return 0;
}
```

43: What is the output? Explain.

```
include<stdio.h>
int numberFun(int counter1) {
    printf(" %d", counter1);
    if (counter1 < 3) {
        numberFun (numberFun (++counter1));
    }
    return counter1;
}

int main() {
    numberFun (1);
    return 0;
}
```

Answer:

The Output will be 1 2 3 3 3.

When the number passed as the parameter to the function numberFun() is less than 3, it calls itself recursively with the incremented the counter. Every time the function is called, the counter is printed. So the main () function calls numberFun(1) with 1 as the parameter, the counter's value 1 is printed on screen. Then since 1 < 3, the recursive function is called numberFun(numberFun(++1)). It increments the value of counter1 to 2 first and prints 2 and again gets into recursion. Again numberFun() is called with ++2 or 3 as the parameter value. This time, since the value of counter1 = 3, it will not satisfy the condition and will return the value of counter1 as 3. Since numberFun(numberFun(++1)) is called inside the function numberFun(), the net effect is numberFun(numberFun(numberFun(3))). Since the function is called 3 times, 3 is printed 3 times. Once the counter1 is 3, the recursion ends.

44: Explain some of the functionalities that can be processed using recursion.

Answer:

Recursive functions are those functions that call themselves. When a process has to repeat itself n times, a recursive function is used instead of an iteration. Recursion helps data hiding. It hides the information regarding the logic applied whereas in iteration, the entire set of code is open for manipulation. Recursive functions are used when you want to solve mathematical equations such as factorials, statistical expressions and any calculations with n repetitive processes.

45: What is recursion in C?

Answer:

Recursion is the method of calling the same function repeatedly till a condition is met. There must be a special condition included in the function to stop the repeated call to the function, or else the function will be called and executed forever

46: What are advantages and disadvantages of using recursion?

Answer:

An advantage of using recursion is the simplicity. The complex coding using iterative statements can be solved in a simple way using recursion.

The disadvantage of using recursion is that every time it is required to save the return address, function parameters, etc., are in the stack for each function call.

Chapter 5

Pointer and its Handling

47: Explain pointer variables and pointer operators in C++.

Answer:

A pointer variable is a variable that stores the address of another variable. It stores the address and using the address, you can access the data stored in that address. A pointer variable is declared as <datatype> *<var_name>. Here the datatype does not mention the datatype of the variable, instead, it is the datatype of the pointer. There are basically 2 types of pointer operators - * and &. * is used to access the value in the address and & is used to access the address. For example,

This code snippet contains an int type variable called val and an int type pointer *ptrval.

```
int val;
int*ptrval;
```

val = 0;

ptrval = &val; // assigns the address of the int val

cout << *ptrval; // prints the value stored in the address on the screen

48: Explain Multiple Indirection in C++.

Answer:

Having a pointer to a pointer in C++ is possible. This is called Multiple Indirection. Normally a pointer contains the address of the variable that it points to. But in Multiple Indirection, one pointer contains the address of another pointer that contains the address of the variable. Even though, multiple indirection can be implemented upto any levels, a pointer to pointer is enough to handle most of the situations. When you have multiple levels of multiple indirections it becomes very difficult to track. A pointer to a pointer must be declared as <datatype> **<pointername>. When you declare a pointer to a pointer as int **pptr, it means that pptr is a pointer to an int pointer rather than pointer to an int.

49: What are the common errors committed while using pointers?

Answer:

Though pointers are used widely in C programming, there are certain commonly committed mistakes when coding with pointers. Some of them are trivial and some are very important features. One such pitfall is not assigning the address of the variable to which it points before using the pointer. A pointer should always point to an address of the variable rather than the value of the variable. Most of the times we tend to forget the fact that *pointer1 and pointer1 are totally different. *pointer1 refers to the value at the address and pointer1 refers to an address. So if you want to assign the pointer to a function, you have to express it such as

pointer1 = (char *) malloc(50) instead of

*pointer1= (char *) malloc(50)

If you want to assign the value, you have to write it as

*pointer1 = 'A';

It is also important to check for Null pointers before a value is assigned.

50: Explain these pointer declarations.

    a)   **int (*pointer1) [3]**

    b)   **(* fn1( )) ( )**

    c)   **int *pointer1[3]**

    d)   **float * (* fn1 [3]) ( )**

    e)   **float (* fn1) ( )**

Answer:

These are different ways in which you can declare a pointer. The declarations are interpreted as below.

    a)   Pointer1 is a pointer to an int array of size 3.

    b)   Function fn1 returns a pointer to a function that returns an int. Since the return type is not specified, by default it is an int.

    c)   Pointer1 is an int pointer array of size 3. It points to integers.

    d)   Fn1 is a pointer array of size 3 to a function that returns a float pointer

e)   Fn1 is a pointer to a function that returns a float.

The position of the * and brackets() determine the variable's type.

51: What is a pointer in C and when a pointer can be referred as a wild pointer?

Answer:

A pointer is a data type which stores the memory address of any type of data item including the address of a pointer data type as well, in which case It is called pointers to pointers.

A wild pointer comes into the picture when previously a pointer stores the address of a data variable, but somehow the data variable has already been deallocated from the memory but the pointer still stores the address of that variable.

52: What is a void pointer?

Answer:

Sometimes it is needed for a single pointer to store the address of another data type variable. In this case, the pointer is not associated with any particular data type while It is being declared. Instead the declaration uses a keyword 'void' to distinguish this pointer from other pointers, and that the void pointer can store address of any other data type variable.

Syntax:

    void * <Ptr_Variable>;

53: What is a NULL pointer?

Answer:

Pointer stores the main memory address of a variable or object, but if the pointer doesn't store address of any variable or object, then it is called a NULL pointer.

54: What is an array of pointers and how it is declared?

Answer:

An array of pointers hold the addresses of a number of variables of the same data type. It is declared as below:

    <Datatype> * <PointerArrayName>[<size of the array>]

55: What is a constant pointer and how is it declared?

Answer:

A pointer holds the memory address of another variable, and at times It is required that the pointer not point to the address of any other variable other than the current one. This is where the constant pointer comes into picture. It is declared by using keyword 'const'.

    <data type> * const <ptr_var>; #ptr_var is a constant pointer

56: How is the pointer to a constant variable declared?

Answer:

A constant pointer and a pointer to a constant variable are two different concepts. A pointer to a constant variable can be declared using keyword 'const'. In this case, the pointer stores the address of a variable whose value can't be changed, but the pointer can carry other variable's memory address.

    const <data type> * <ptr_var>;

57: Where can near and far pointers be used?

Answer:

The use of near or far pointers depend on the memory model being used by the program. If it is required to store only the offset part of the address, then a near pointer of size 2 bytes is used. If it is required to store both the segment and the offset part of the address, then a far pointer of size 4 bytes is used.

58: What is the syntax for declaring a far pointer?

Answer:

The keyword 'far' is used while declaring a far pointer as in the following example:

    <datatype> far <pointer_var_name>;

Example:

    int far ptr_int;

59: Explain, using an example, how constant pointer and pointer to constant variable are different.

Answer:

In the case of constant pointer, the pointer can't carry address of any other variable, but it can change the contents at the address (the value of the variable). In the case of pointer to constant variable, the concept is reversed. The pointer can contain the address of any other variable, but it can't change the content at the address (the value of the variable). Consider the example below:

    int a =10; int b =20;

Now suppose address of variable 'a' is 10004.

    Int * const ptr = &a;

In this example, the statement '*ptr=30;' is fine since the pointer contents is being changed (no compiler error). The statement 'ptr=&b' will generate a complier error since the value of a constant is being changed.

60: How is constant pointer declared so it doesn't allow the variable's content or value to be changed?

Answer:

This is done by combining the concept of both constant pointer as well as pointer to a constant object or variable. The syntax for this is as follows:

const <data type> * const <ptr_variable> = &<variablename>

It is important to note that initialization has to be done at the time of definition.

61: Explain the output of the following program.

```
void main (){
    int *ptr, a[][3] = {12,32,45,67,89,90};
    ptr = a + 1;
    printf ("%d %d", *(ptr+1), *ptr+1) ;
}
```

Answer:

The output will be 89 68, since in the first case *(ptr+1), the pointer was increased before dereference, so it holds the next address during the times of dereference. In the second case *ptr+1, the pointer is de-referenced first, then the de-referenced value is incremented by one.

62: Explain the output of the following program.

```
void main () {
        int * ptr;
        *ptr = 45; # or int b; *ptr = &b;
        }
```

Answer:

The above program throws the runtime error 'Null Pointer Assignment'. The pointer variable 'ptr' is declared, but it is never assigned an address of an integer variable. So, 'ptr' is not pointing to any specific memory location. When it tries to store a value in the memory location ptr is pointing to, it throws runtime error.

63: Explain the output of the following program.

```
    void main () {
        int X [] = {10,20,30,40,50};
        int *ptr = X+3;
        printf("%d", *ptr);
            }
```

Answer:

The output will be 30, since ptr is assigned the address of X[3].Here X refers to the base address of the 1D array and X+3 refers to the address of X[3]. The * ptr is the value held at the pointer address.

64: How is a pointer defined to a function and how is function called using the pointer variable?

Answer:

A pointer to a function variable carries the starting address of the function. To define a pointer to a function, It is mandatory to know the return type of the function and the arguments types being passed to the function. One pointer variable can carry the starting address of more than one function as long as the return type and argument type in the definition of the pointer to function matches with signature of the function. The syntax to define pointer to function:

<ReturnTypeOfFunction> (*<Ptr_to_Function_Name>) (<argumentTypes separated with commas>);

Suppose there is a method:

int Calculate(int x, int y, int z);

Then pointer to this function can be defined as:

int (*Ptr_calculate) (int,int,int)

Ptr_calculate = Calculate

The function can be called using the pointer to function as:

int result = (*Ptr_calculate)(a,b,c)

65: What is dangling reference in C and when is it a factor?
Answer:

A dangling reference is a factor when a pointer carries the address of a data variable, but the data itself no longer exists in memory. For example, the data has already been deallocated from memory, so the pointer points to a unallocated memory location.

66: What is garbage memory and when does it come into picture?
Answer:

Initially, a pointer is carrying the address of a data type. If for some reason the pointer is released from memory there is no way to retrieve the value of the data. So the data value lies in the memory till the program ends or the function that defined it goes out of scope. This abandoned at memory is called garbage memory.

67: In terms of the pointer, what is indirection or dereference operator?

Answer:

Pointer stores the memory address of a variable. When the code accesses the value stored in that memory address, it is required to use '*', or indirection operator, with the pointer variable to access the value in the memory address help by the pointer.

Example:

int * <Ptr_Variable>; int a;

Ptr_Variable = &a;

printf("Value of a = %d", *Ptr_Variable); #prints the value of variable 'a'

68: What is the address operator in relation to the pointer in C?

Answer:

A pointer holds the memory address of a variable or object. The content of the memory at that address is the value of the variable. Use the address operator ('&') to load the variable memory address into the pointer variable. Use the address operator as follows:

Int * <ptr_variable>, item;

ptr_variable = &item; #Now the memory address of variable 'item' is assigned

69: What will be the value of the following program and explain why.

```
void main () {
    char arr[] = "Hello";
    char * ptr = arr;
    printf("%s", ++ptr);
}
```

Answer:

The output will be the string "ello" not "Hello". Since the specifier "%s" always accepts an address and then prints the strings from that address till the end. In the program above, the address is passed to printf while the address of arr[1] is pre-incrementing the pointer, so it will start printing the string from the letter 'e'.

70: Explain the output of the following program.

```
void main () {
    int X[3][2] = {{10,20},{30,40},{50,60}};
    printf("%d ", ***(X+1));
}
```

Answer:

The program will generate the error 'Invalid indirection in function main', since for a 2D array dereference operators can be used up to two levels but after that it gets consumed. In the above case **(X+1) refers to integer 30, now a dereference operator can't be used over an integer, so the program can't be executed.

71: Explain the output of the following program.

```
void main () {
    char arr[5] = {1,2,3,4,5};
    printf ("%d %d", 3[arr]);
    }
```

Answer:

Output will be 3. Many of you might be expecting an error to be thrown. But arr[3] and 3[arr] are same. The internal representation for arr[3] is *(arr+3) and internal representation for 3[arr] is *(3+arr). So, 3[arr] will give the same output as that would have been given by arr[3].

Chapter 6

Templates

72: What is a template in C++?

Answer:

We can create generic functions in C++ that are called Templates.
The main advantage of using a template is that, the same function
can be used with any data type of parameters. This is made
possible by declaring the function with the data type as one of the
parameters. So the user passes the data as well as the data type of
the value passed to the function. The compiler will create as many
copies of the generic function based on the data types used and
accordingly choose the right one to process a particular function
call. This is like implicit function overloading. For Example, the
function for swapping 2 variable values can be declared as:

template <class XY> void swapThem(XY &ab, XY &cd) {

    XY tempVar;

    tempVar = ab;

```
ab = bc;
bc = tempVar;
}
```

73: Why do we need templates in C++?

Answer:

Templates in C++ can be used for many important purposes. Since they are generic functions, they can be used to create type-safe stacks. Templates reduce the code. Since Templates can handle all data types, you can create any type of collection class using a Template. They are also used to implement smart pointers to hide the operator overriding techniques. Templates being classes, encapsulate the operator overriding details. You can also implements extra type-checking with templates. Even though these functionalities can be implemented in many other ways also, Templates are much preferred as it is a write-once-work-with-all-datatypes method. They are easier to understand and help encapsulation. Since the compiler can determine the data type during compile time, Templates are more typesafe.

74: What is the syntax of declaring a function template?

Answer:

The syntax for declaring a function template is as follows:

```
template <class P, class Q, . . . >
<return_dataType> <func_name> (<arg1,<arg2, ... >>)
{--- func body ---
}
```

75: What is the syntax for declaring a class template?

Answer:

The syntax for declaring a class template is as follows:

    template <class P, class Q, . . . >

    class <name_of_class>

    { P p1, Q q1, ... ;

    P <fun_name> (P p11, Q q11);

    <other functions involving template data types>

    }

This page is intentionally left blank.

Chapter 7

General Concepts

76: What are the three basic concepts of C++?

Answer:

C++ supports object oriented programming. The main 3 concepts that come with C++ are those of Classes & Objects, Inheritance and Polymorphism. We can create classes in C++. A class is like a structure that forms the framework of an entity. The class contains member variables and member functions. The member variables can contain the characteristics of the entity and the member functions define the functionality of the entity. Objects are instances of the class or the actual entities. Every object will have the characteristics and functionalities as defined in the class. Inheritance is the feature that lets a class derive the functionality of a base class. The common functionalities are defined in a base class and other classes will derived from this base class. It basically implements the IS A relationship. Polymorphism in C++

means that a function can be implemented in different ways in different classes and which function has to be executed is decided based on the object that class it. For example, if the base class has a function A implemented in one way and the derived classes B & C have implemented A in 2 different ways, then when base class object calls the function A it functions according to its definition in the base class. When the derived class B calls the function A it functions according to its definition in class B and when C.A() is called, it works according to its definition in C.

77: Explain Preprocessing in C++.

Answer:

Preprocessing makes your source code readable to the compiler. As the name suggests, before the compiler processes your source code, it goes through a trimming process wherein the comments and are replaced by a space and codes that end with the next line or '\n' are added to the next line to form a single line of code. This makes the source code more readable to the compiler. Other than cleaning up the code, the pre-processor processes all the directives that start with # in the program. It includes the files mentioned in the #include. It will replace the macro names with their definition that start with #define wherever the macros are accessed. It also decodes the conditional compilation directives that start with #if.

78: What are the different ways in which the static keyword is used?

Answer:

In C++, the keyword *static* can be used to create static variables inside a function, static objects, static member variables or static member functions. Static variables in a function are used to store data that can be accessed uniformly across the program. They are initialized only once even if the program calls the function many times. This makes sure the data stored in the static variable is not lost with each call. When you create a static object, the scope of the object remains till the end of the program. Even if you have created the static object inside a function or a block of code, once created, it remains in the static memory till the program exits. Static member variables of a class can be accessed outside the class. Once the data member is declared static inside the class, it has to be initialized outside the class. It cannot be declared again anywhere in the program. The value of the static member variables can be accessed throughout the program without having an object. Static member variables and functions are accessed directly with the syntax <classname>::<membername>. Static member functions cannot access the normal data members and variables. It can access only other static members and variables.

79: Have a look at the following program. Explain whether it will compile and execute in both C & C++.

```
#include <stdio.h>
int main(void) {
    newFunction();
}
int newFunction() {
    printf("You are in New Function!!!");
    return 0;
```

}

Answer:

The program will compile and run without any errors in C because even if newFunction() is not declared before it is called, the compiler will run a check for it within the program and compile the program. Once compiled, it will have the reference for the function and hence, will run. But in C++, you have to declare the function before it is being called. Hence, the C++ compiler will throw an error when you try to compile this function. If you move the function declaration above the main function or before the function is called, the C++ compiler will happily compile the program.

80: What is source code and object code in C?
Answer:

Source code is written by a programmer using a text editor in a high level language meaning the programming terms and statements are understandable by a human. By convention, the Source code in C has a 'c' file extension. Source code is compiled (using a compiler) to create the object code – hexadecimal instructions that can be carried out by the processor. The extension of Object code in C is '.obj' in Windows or '.o' in UNIX. From the object code, the final executable (.exe) can be produced by using the linker, loader etc.

81: What are command line arguments?
Answer:

Command line arguments are input variables accepted by a C

program when it is called or invoked.

82: What is the use of header file in C? Use the example of stdio.h to explain a header file.

Answer:

Most of the times, header files carry the prototype or declaration of a library function. For example, when a programmer is using printf () function in a program, then the prototype of that function should be declared at the start of the program as normally functions are defined by the programmer and the function prototype is written at the start of the program. For library functions like printf(), their prototypes have already been declared in header files like stdio.h. Apart from carrying prototypes of predefined library functions, the header file contains constants and macros as well.

The advantage of using header files is that frequently used or common functions do not have to define the prototype of that function every time at the start of the module. They can be declared in a header file, then only the header file has to be included. All the functions, constants defined in header are now defined in the module, and easily included in other modules.

83: What is the difference if a header file is included in C in the following two ways?

    a)   #include <header file>

    b)   #include "header file"

Answer:

    a)   For a header file included with #include <header file>, the compiler only searches the header file in the 'include' directory (the standard search path for header files in C).

b) When #include "header file" is used, the compiler first searches for the header file in the current directory where the C file resides. Then the compiler will search the standard search path ('include' directory).

84: What is the role of linker in C?

Answer:

After the compiler produces files containing machine understandable object code, the linker takes those object files along with predefined library functions used in the program and produces the final executable file. Now the executable file can be executed using loader.

85: What is the maximum value for a 16 bit integer in both signed and unsigned case?

Answer:

An integer of 16 bits in the unsigned case has a maximum value of 65535.The signed case has a maximum value of 32767, since one bit is reserved for the sign identification. The formula to calculate the maximum value is pow(2,16)-1 in unsigned case.

86: Explain the output of the following program.

```
void stack_function (int X, int Y)
    {
    printf ('%d %d', X, Y);
    }
```

```
void main () {
    int c = 12;
    stack_function( c++ , c) ;
        }
```

Answer:

The output will be 13 12 rather than 13 13. Since the parameters are passed to a function and stored in stack area, the rule for stack is the push operation happens from right to left and the pop operation from left to right.

87: How does the preprocessing stage aid in getting executable code from a source C file?

Answer:

Before source code is sent to the compiler, putting it through the preprocessor prepares it for compilation. The functionalities provided by this preprocessing stage includes substitution facilities (Macros), File inclusion (#include), and Conditional compilation.

88: What is NULL value in C?

Answer:

NULL value is also denoted by '\0', whose ASCII value is 0(zero). To mark end of a string in C, a NULL value is used as a terminating character in a string.

89: What is strict type checking in C++ and what is its advantage?

Answer:

Strict type checking involves the functions in a program. If a function is defined in C++, then its prototype is mandatory even if the function call is made after the definition of function. In C it is not compulsory for the function call to be made after the function definition. The advantage of having a mandatory prototype is that there is a data type compatibility check by the compiler during the function call to verify the actual parameters being passed matches the data types mentioned in the function definition.

90: Explain the output of the following program.

```
void main() {
    char ch = 'A';
    printf("%d", ch) ;
        }
```

Answer:

The output will be 65, the ASCII value of 'A', since in memory a character is stored as its ASCII value. In this program an integer specifier (%d) is used rather than a char specifier(%c) for a character variable. Hence, the program's output will be 65 rather than 'A'.

Chapter 8

Control Flow Statements

91: What is the difference between a switch and if-else?

Answer:

A switch case is used when the variable has to be checked against a set of fixed values. For example,

```
int choice = 0;
cout << "Input your choice ";
cin >> choice;
switch (choice) {
case 0:
    count<<"Choice is 0";
case 1
    count<<"Choice is 1";
case 2
    count<<"Choice is 2";
case 3
```

```
count<<"Choice is 3";
default:
        count<<"Choice is Default";
}
```

In this case, the value of choice is checked against each case irrespective of whether the previous condition was met or not. So in the above example, choice will be checked against all 4 options and then default will also be executed.

An if-else construct works in a different way. When there are multiple options to be checked, the if - else if construct is used. But when once the condition is met, it comes out of the if block.

```
If (choice==0)
        count<<"Choice is 0";
else if (choice == 1)
        count<<"Choice is 1";
else if (choice == 2)
        count<<"Choice is 2";
else if (choice == 3)
        count<<"Choice is 3";
else
        count<<"Choice out of bound";
}
```

In this case, as soon as the value of choice is found on one of the else conditions, the control shifts outside the if-else block to the next statement of the program after the if-else block.

92: What are the different types of loops available in C++ and

when are they used?

Answer:

C++ offers 4 different loops in the programs. They are the while loop, for loop, do while loop and nested loops. The while loops are used to perform the set of instructions till the condition is true. The for loop will perform the instructions within the code block for a set number of times. The do while loop will be executed at least once and then the condition is checked. Nested loops can be used, one inside the other.

```
while (<condition>) {
}
```

```
for(initial value; condition; increment / decrement) {
}
```

```
do {
} while (<condition>)
```

```
for(initial value1; condition1; increment / decrement) {
    for(initial value2; condition2; increment / decrement) {
    }
}
```

93: How do break and continue statements differ from each other?

Answer:

Both statements are used inside a loop, but they have a different purpose. When a break statement is encountered, the program breaks out of the loop. It skips to the very next program statement after the loop. A continue statement causes the program to skip the remaining programming statements in the loop and re-begins execution from the start of the loop. Program execution remains in the loop.

94: What is the difference between while and do-while loop?
Answer:
Both the loops are used where a certain set of statements are executed repeatedly as long as the condition provided in the loop is met. But they differ the way this condition is placed in the loop construct. In a while loop, first the condition is checked and if true it proceeds to execute the statements in the loop. In a do-while loop, the condition is not checked before executing the statements for the first iteration. Only after the executing the loop statements is the condition checked and returns to the loop if true.

With the do-while loop, the statements inside the loop are executed at least once.

95: Write the syntax of while and do-while loop.
Answer:
Syntax of while:
While (condition)
    {
    Loop body
    }

Syntax of do-while:

do

{

Loop body

} while (condition) ;

96: What is the purpose of using 'default' keyword in a switch construct?

Answer:

A switch statement takes one expression (an integer, character, or constant) whose value is compared against the case value. When the expression output doesn't match any of the case values; any statements under the (optional) default part of the switch construct are executed.

97: When is the switch statement preferred over if-else statements?

Answer:

Usually logic done through multiple if-else statements can be implemented using switch statement. The logic of a switch statement is usually more clear and direct and more readable as source code than multiple if-else statements.

98: What is goto statement in C?

Answer:

If, if-else, switch are all conditional branch statements. The goto will cause the program to start executing from a particular labeled statement unconditionally.

<label_name>: statement;

```
goto <label_name>;
```

99: What is the syntax for 'if' and 'if-else' statements?

Answer:

'if' syntax:

```
if (<condition>)
    {
    <statements_if_condition_True>;
    }
```

'if-else' syntax:

```
if (<condition_1>)
    {
    <Statements_if_block>;
    }
else
    {
    <Statement_else_block>
    }
```

100: Classify the different control flow statements in C/C++.

Answer:

Control flow statements refer to looping and branching statements. Control flow statements are if, if-else, switch, goto, for, while, and do-while statements. Among the 7 statements, the first four statements are branching statements.

101: Explain the output of the following program.

void main ()

```
    {
int a = 30;
Switch (a){
    case 12:
        printf ('1st case block');
        break;
    default:
        printf("default block");
        }
    }
```

Answer:

The Output will be "default block" since there is no matching case block for the value accepted by the switch argument.

102: Explain the output of the following program.

```
    void main() {
        int n=1;
        for (; ;)
        printf("Hello world");
        }
```

Answer:

The output will be the string "Hello World" an infinite number of times. In the program above the loop doesn't have any conditions, hence the printf() statement in the for loop will run infinite times.

This page is intentionally left blank.

Chapter 9

Data Types, Variables and Operators

103: What is the use of the extern keyword?

Answer:

The extern keyword is used to make the variables and functions more visible in the program. It is more useful when used with variables since functions are generally globally visible within the program. The extern keyword is used only to declare the variable and it has to be defined and initialized separately. Declaration can be done any number of times, but definition can be done only once in a program.

extern int numVar; - this is the declaration outside the main function

int numVar; - this is the definition inside the main function

numVar = 0; - this is the initialization which is also done inside the main

extern int numVar = 0; - this is also a valid statement. In fact, it is equivalent to all 3 required actions; declaration, definition and initialization.

104: What are local and global variables?

Answer:

Local variables are local to the context where they are declared. If a variable is declared inside a function, it is local to the function and cannot be accessed anywhere outside the function. Similarly, if a variable is declared inside a block of code or inside an if – else condition, it is local to that block only. Global variables are declared outside the blocks and hence, they are accessible throughout the program. Typically, the global variables are declared just below the header files so that they are available throughout the program. A program can have a local as well as a global variable with the same name. But the local variable will be given preference when found inside a block. Local variables are to be explicitly initialized. Global variables are automatically initialized with the default initializer value.

105: When you pass a variable value to a function, what is the difference between passing by value and passing by reference?

Answer:

When you pass by value, you are only sending a copy of your program's variable to the function. But when you are passing by reference, you are directly passing the address inside the memory and letting the function access the address where the data is stored. When the function can directly access the physical address of the variable, it fetches the data and sometimes even changes it. Pointers are used to pass by reference and normal variables or anonymous variables are used to pass by value. The function only accesses the value passed and never attempts to change the value as the value passed is only a copy.

106: What is the difference between static and global variables?

Answer:

a) A global variable is defined outside all functions in a module, where a static variable can be declared either inside a function or inside a block or outside of all functions.

b) If a static variable is defined inside a particular block or inside a function, then the scope of the static variable is limited to that block or function, whereas the extent of the global variable is throughout the program execution.

c) With a global variable, the scope remains throughout the module. If it is externally defined using extern keyword, then its scope is extended to the other modules as well, its extent remains throughout the program execution.

d) Static variables are declared using a static keyword. The distinction of a global variable can only be known by the point of declaration of the variable.

107: What is a register variable and when it can be used?

Answer:

A register variable is a special type of variable where memory is allocated in the CPU registers. It can be declared by using the keyword 'register'.

The advantage of declaring a register for a frequently employed variable is to speed up the execution of the program. The number of register variables in a program is limited. When compiler cannot allocate a register variable due to limited availability of CPU registers, then the variable is allocated as auto variable.

108: What are external variables and where they can be used?
Answer:

When the program requires sharing a variable defined in one module with other modules, then an external variable is used. Before creating an external variable, a global is created in any of the modules, then other modules needing to share the global variable can declare the same global variable again in their modules using 'extern' keyword. In this way, all other modules can access the value of the global variable and the global variable has to be declared only once. In the other modules the global variable is declared with a preceding 'extern'.

109: What is the scope of a variable?
Answer:

The scope of a variable defines from which part of the program the variable can be accessed or used. A variable can't be used outside its scope. For a global variable, the scope is throughout the whole module, but for a local variable the scope is limited to the block where it is defined.

110: What is the difference between the way variables are defined in C and C++?

Answer:

It is compulsory that local variables have to be defined at the start of a block or a function or a program in C, where as in C++, the local variables can be defined at any point inside a block or a function giving the flexibility to the programmer to declare and use the variable at any point.

111: What is operator overloading and how it can be achieved?

Answer:

Operator overloading is one form of polymorphism where the operators can be implemented on user defined data types apart from standard data types. For example, there is no way to add two complex data types since there is not a standard complex data type. So to add or subtract two complex data types, which are defined by the user, can be done by overloading the operators. The overloading of operators is achieved by using normal member functions of a class as well as using friend functions.

112: Where can the scope resolution operator be used in C++?

Answer:

When two variables are declared with the same name, one as a local variable and another as a global variable inside a module, to access the global variable from the block where the local variable is present, the programmer uses the scope resolution operator. This operator is denoted by '::'. The global variable that needs to be accessed inside the local block is prefixed with the scope resolution operator, whereas the local variable is accessed conventionally.

113: How unary and binary operators are different in C?
Answer:
A unary operator always operates on a single operand. For example, increment(++) / decrement(--) always acts upon a single operand.

A binary operator always requires two operands to allow the execution of the statement. For example, addition(+) or subtraction(-) operator must have two operands to have a resulting sum or difference.

114: What is ternary operator and what syntax is used to write it?
Answer:
When a choice is required between two options a ternary operator (also called conditional operator) can be used (similar to an if-else statement).
Syntax:

<Condition> ? <expression_A> : <expression_B>
When this statement is encountered by the compiler, then expression A is evaluated if the condition is True, else expression B is used.

115: What are increment and decrement operators? What is the syntax of using them?
Answer:
These are unary operators for incrementing ('++') or decrementing

('--') the value of variables.

Syntax:

    <Variable> ++ or ++ <Variable>

    <Variable> -- or -- <Variable>

116: What is the value of a and b after the code execution and why?

    void question()

        {

        Int x= 5 ; int y ;

        y = x++ ;

        }

Answer:

The value of x will be 6 as expected, but the value of y will be 5, not 6. The value of x is 6 due to the postfix increment operator, which incremented the x AFTER the equal operation. So the value of y is 5.

117: What is lifetime of a variable?

Answer:

The variable lifetime is the time through which a variable remains available in memory during a program.

118: What is the output of the following code? Explain.

    void question()

        {

        Int x=5, y=0, z=9, w;

        w = (y++, x++, y--, z++, ++x);

```
    printf("%d", w);
    }
```

Answer:

The output will be 7, the value of 'x', since it is incremented twice and it is the last operation so it will be assigned to the value of 'w'. All the expressions enclosed within comma operator are evaluated from left to right.

119: What does 'sizeof' function return?

Answer:

This function returns the size of an expression, variable, or data type in bytes. The input to this function can be a user defined data type as well.

sizeof(<data type>) or sizeof(<variable>) or
sizeof(<expression>)

120: How does the meaning of increment or decrement operators change when used as prefix or postfix?

Answer:

When the increment (++) or decrement (--) operator is used as a prefix (++<Variable> / --<Variable>), first the variable is incremented or decremented and then the value is used in the expression.

When the increment or decrement is a used as a postfix (<Variable>++/ <Variable>--), the value of the variable is used in the expression, then its value is incremented or decremented.

121: What arithmetic operators are present in C++?

Answer:

There are a total of 7 arithmetic operators (including unary and binary. The unary operators are unary plus(+), unary minus(-) and the binary operators are addition(+), subtraction(-), multiplication(*), division(/), modulus(%).

If programmer wants to use arithmetic operators on 'user defined data types', then operator overloading mechanism has to be implemented.

122: Classify the different data types present in C.

Answer:

Generally there are three data types; fundamental data types, user defined data types, and derived types. Fundamental data types are integer, floating point number, and character. Derived data types include functions, pointers, and arrays. The user defined data types are union, structure, and enum.

123: What is a relational operator? What different types of relational operators are present in C?

Answer:

A relational operator is used when making comparisons between two expressions. Generally, this operator is used with 'if' statements. There are 6 relational operators and all are binary. The different types of relational operators present in C are: less than (<); less than or equal to(<=); greater than(>); greater than or equal to(>=); equal to(==); and not equal to(!=).

When an expression carries relational operators, then the expression always returns an integer to be used in the 'if' statement.

124: What is a logical operator? What logical operators are available in C?

Answer:

A logical operator is used when the programmer wants to mix more than one condition. There are 3 logical operators (two binary and one unary) in C: logical and (&&); logical or (||); and logical not (!). The '&&' operator will be true when both expressions around the '&&' are true. The '||' operator will be true if either one of the expressions present around the '||' are true. The unary '!' operator negates an expression.

125: How are logical and (&&) and logical or (||) operators are executed in an expression?

Answer:

If there are two sub expressions which apply a logical and ('&&'), then the evaluation of the 2nd operation depends upon the outcome of the 1st expression, so if the 1st expression evaluates to be False, then the 2nd expression will not be executed. But if the 1st expression evaluates to be True, then the 2nd expression will be executed.

Similarly, for a logical or ('||'), if an expression implements this operator over two sub expressions, then the execution of 2nd expression depends on the outcome of the 1st expression. If 1st expression evaluates to True, then 2nd execution will not be executed, else the 2nd expression will be executed.

126: What is sign qualifier? What is the syntax of declaring it for an integer?

Answer:

The sign qualifier is a form of qualifier that changes the behavior of a variable, whether the variable carries positive or negative numbers. There are 'signed' and 'unsigned' qualifiers. Singed qualifiers make the variable carry both positive and negative numbers. The 'unsigned' qualifier makes the variable carry only positive numbers.

When no sign qualifier is mentioned for a variable, the default is to make the variable a 'signed' qualifier.

Syntax:

    <signed or unsigned> int <variable_name>;

127: What is a size qualifier? How an integer can be declared of such type?

Answer:

The size qualifier is a form of qualifier that changes the size of a variable. They are 'short' and 'long'. For example, the size of a short int is 2 bytes, whereas size of a long int is 4 bytes.

Syntax:

    <long or short> int <variable_name>;

128: What is bit-wise operator? List the available bit-wise operators in C++.

Answer:

If an individual or number of bits from a word needs to be altered or shifted, then a bit-wise operator is used. Bit-wise operators include: bitwise and (&); bitwise or (|); bitwise EX-OR (^); shift left (<<); shift right (>>); and bitwise complement (~). The bitwise complement is a unary operator.

129: How does a bitwise complement operator work?
Answer:

Since the bitwise complement operator is an unary operator, it only takes one argument as its operand. Then, it reverses all the bits of the operand i.e. when a bit in a word is '0' after bitwise complement operator it becomes '1'.

130: How does a bitwise shift operators work?
Answer:

Since the bitwise shift operators are binary operators, so require two operands as their input. The first operand is the variable which needs to be shifted and the second operand provides how many bits the 1st operand will be shifted. While shifting the bits in the operand, the bits moved out are replaced with zeros.
Example:

int a = 48; int b = a << 3;
Int a = 35; int b = a>>3;

131: What is a variable in C?
Answer:

When a variable is defined, then a location in main memory is combined with the variable name, which stores data of a particular data type. Over the course of execution of the program, a variable can be different values - unlike a constant which is always the same value. A variable can be of any data type including standard data types like int, char, etc., or it can a user defined data type as well.

132: What rules do programmers need to follow while naming a variable in C?

Answer:

The followings rules apply while assigning variable names:

a) The variable name can carry only letters (A-Z, a-z), digits (0-9) and underscore (_)

b) The variable name must begin with a letter or an underscore

c) Variable name cannot be a reserved keyword

d) Variable names should not exceed 31 characters

e) Variable names are case sensitive (the same name in different combinations of upper case and lower case characters will be separate variables)

133: Why are variables declared?

Answer:

Declaring a variable serves two main purposes:

a) During declaration of a variable the type of data the variable is going to hold is known to the compiler

b) A name is associated to the variable so that variable can be easily accessed using this name

134: How is a variable declared so that its value can't be altered in the program once an initial value is assigned?

Answer:

To have a variable in the program whose value can't be changed, the programmer needs to use 'const' keyword, so that it makes the variable a constant, and its value can't be altered.

    const <datatype> <variable_name>;

135: What is operator precedence?

Answer:

Operator precedence defines the order operators are used in an expression, and it follows typical algebraic precedence. For example, the expression 'a+b*c' is evaluated as 'a+(b*c)' according to the operator precedence rule (since multiplication takes precedence over addition).

136: What is operator associativity while evaluating an expression?

Answer:

When an expression involves the same operator used multiple times, then the associativity rule is applied. For example, the expression 'a+b-c', has the same operator precedence, so the associativity for these operators is from 'Left to Right'; hence the expression will be evaluated as '(a+b)-c'.

137: What is type conversion?

Answer:

Type conversion involves converting the current data type of a variable to a different data type. Generally it is either implicit or explicit type conversion depending upon the way the data type is converted by the compiler or by the programmer.

138: What is implicit type conversion? Use an example to explain it.

Answer:

This type conversion is automatically done by compiler when it finds different data types involved in an expression. For example – when a division occurs between a float data type and an integer type i.e. (float/int), then 'int' is automatically converted to type 'floating point number' before the division happens.

Implicit type conversion is also called as 'automatic type conversion'.

139: What are the different ways implicit type conversion can be done?

Answer:

Implicit type conversion takes the type conversion from higher to lower data type or from lower to higher data types - called 'promotion' and 'demotion'. Promotion is where a lower data type gets converted to a higher data type, for example with (float/int) 'int' gets converted to 'float', which is a higher data type than integer. In case of demotion, the reverse happens, i.e. higher data type like float gets converted to lower data type like int.

140: What is explicit type conversion?

Answer:

This type of type conversion comes in handy, when the programmer wants to do a different data type conversion than the compiler default conversion. This can be achieved through 'type casting'. Both higher to lower and lower to higher data type conversions are done with explicit conversion.

141: How does separation by comma operator affect the evaluation of expressions?

Answer:

The evaluation of expressions always happens from left to right where comma operator is used, but the final output of the comma separated expressions is the value of the last expression.

142: What will the output be of the following program and explain why? (Integer size is 2 bytes.)

```
void main () {
    int i;
    signed int n=32767;
    for (i=1; i<n;i++)
        printf("%d", i);
}
```

Answer:

The output will be 1..32767,-32768,-32767,..0,1..., and so on in an infinite loop. Since n is a signed integer of size 2 bytes its maximum value is 32767. In the for loop, when i reaches the value 32767, then its incremented value becomes -32768 and this value is less than 32767, hence there will be an infinite loop of values ranging from -32768 to 32767.

143: Explain the output of the following program. (The integer is

of size 2 bytes)

```
void main () {
    signed int X = 32767;
    int y = X+1, z = X+1;
    printf("%d %d", y , z);
    }
```

Answer:

The output will be -32768 -32767. The integer is of size 16 bits (2 bytes). In the above program, X already carries the maximum value of a signed integer, so if it is incremented it will roll over to the very minimum value (-32768) and begin incrementing (-32767, -32766, ...).

144: What is will be the value of a and b in the function 'func_static' after the for loop in main function is executed till its looping condition is specified? Explain why.

```
void func_static () {
    static int a=1;
    int b = 1;
    a++;b++;
    }
void main () {
    int i;
    for (i=1; i<=5;i++)
        func_static();
    }
```

Answer:

The value of static variable "a" will be 6 and the value of "b" will be 2. A static variable retains their value between function calls but a local variable doesn't.

145: What operators cannot be overloaded?

Answer:

The operators not allowed to be overloaded (unlike other operators such as 'new') are; arithmetic operators, sizeof(), ternary operator, scope resolution operator(: :), member access operator(.), pointer to member(*).

Chapter 10

Macros, typedef, enum

146: What are the advantages of using a typedef?

Answer:

A Typedef is a named alias for an existing data type in C. It is usually used when a data type which is complex in nature is used repeatedly or to give a more meaningful name to a data type for better readability of the code. Sometimes it even helps in platform independent coding when the typedef alias used is named with the size of the data type. This makes it clear to the programmer as to what is the size of the variable used. It can even hide the actual details of the program from the end user.

For example:

typedef unsigned int intVal;

intVal a;

147: What is the difference between a typedef and macro?

Answer:

Typedef defines a new datatype based on an existing data type. This is used to create more meaningful names to the data types that are easier to read in the program. Macros are a named statement or block of code that can be used repeatedly. You can even name a value using a macro whereas typedef can only be an alias name for an existing data type. While the typedef is processed by the compiler, the macros are taken in by the pre-processor and the compiler stops at the call of the macro if it comes across any error while executing the macro. The typedef follows the scope rules, that is, it is local to the block in which it is defined. But the macros, once defined, will be identified by the pre-processor and will be replaced by the macro code wherever they are used irrespective of the scope.

148: What is an enumerated data type and where can it be used?

Answer:

Enumeration comes into the picture when the programmer wants to attach integers to strings. Since this data type is defined by the user, it can contain any number of strings and all of them are assigned a particular integer. This is useful to create a limited set of strings like all the days in a week. An enumerated data type of seven elements naming Monday, Tuesday, etc, can have these values compared as an integer in conditional statements.

149: What is typedef and write its syntax?

Answer:

A typedef is used to create alias names for better understanding the code and for convenience to the programmer of giving special names to the already predefined standard data types.

Syntax:

typedef <existingTypename> <newTypename>

And for pointer and reference variable, the syntax is a bit different:

Typedef < existingTypename> <* or &> < newTypename >

150: What is a macro in C and how is it defined?

Answer:

Macros are special identifiers used to carry the meaning for a constant value. They are defined using preprocessor directive, hence their reference throughout the program is resolved in preprocessing stage. The syntax is:

#define <Macro_identifier> <constant>

Example:

#define True 1

151: What is the advantage of having macro function in a program and how is it defined?

Answer:

Macro function is defined using a preprocessor directive, then the replacement of the function body throughout the program happens in preprocessing stage. Since macro functions are inserted into program there is no passing arguments to called functions, reducing overhead of context-switch and increasing the speed of program execution.

#define <Macro_function> (<parameters>) <function_body>

Example:

#define MultiplicationOfTwoNumbers (x,y) (x*y)

Chapter 11

Library Functions

152: What is the difference between exit() and abort() functions in C?

Answer:

The exit() function systematically exits the program after closing all the open files, flushing the buffer clear, removing any temporary files and also returns an exit status whether or not the exit was successful. When you call an exit() function, it performs any instructions specified in the atexit() function. The exit() is an elegant way of exiting the program. The abort() abruptly ends the program. It does not bother to close the open files or delete the temporary files created by the program. It will not perform the instructions given in the atexit() function. In fact, it will just abort the program. The only way to handle an abort() is to include a SIGABRT signal handler.

153: How do you execute a system command from a C program?

Answer:

We can use the library function system() to run any system command from within the program. For example, if we want to execute the DIR command from the C program, just follow the pattern:

Char strCommand[100];

strcpy(strCommand,"Dir");

system (strCommand);

This will print the list of files and directories in the current directory from where you are running the program. It will function similar to the Dir command given at the command prompt of your desktop. You can use the same method to invoke any program or command from the program.

154: What are the prototypes of printf() and scanf() in C and what do printf and scanf return?

Answer:

Prototype for printf method:

    int printf(const char *format [,argument,.]);

Prototype of scanf method:

    int scanf(const char *format [,...,]);

Printf returns the number of characters printed and scanf returns the numbers of input characters read.

155: Explain the output of the following. (The input given by the

end user is, "Are you ready.")
>   void main () {
>   char PQR [50];
>   scanf("%s", PQR);
>   printf("%s", PQR);
>   }

Answer:

The output will be the string "Are", not the string "Are you ready" since the scanf() library function only reads characters until a white space is encountered. In this example, the string "Are you ready" is entered by the end user. That means scanf will read "Are" and stop since a white space character is present. The variable "PQR" will hold only "Hello".

156: What is the difference between getch() and getche() if both can read a character?

Answer:

The getch() function reads one character from the keyboard but doesn't echo the input character to the screen. The getche() function reads one character from the keyboard and echoes it to the screen.

157: How scanf() and gets() differ from each other in reading strings from an end user in C?

Answer:

scanf() uses '%s' format modifier to read the input until there is a white space character. Conversely, gets() reads certain white space characters including spaces, tabs and it returns when a new line is encountered. Programmers use gets() to capture a multiple word string.

158: What is the output of following code and why?

```
void question()
    {
    Int x [] = {99,11,22,33,44};
    Printf( "M=%d", printf ( "N=%dO=%d", x[3], x[4]) );
    }
```

Answer:

The output will be N=33O=44M=6. Here, the output of N=33 and O=44 is obvious, but the M= part is tricky. The output of M=6 is due to the fact that the printf function will always return the number of characters printed to the output so far.

Chapter 12

Arrays

159: Explain array traversing using pointers.

Answer:

Here's a C program that takes in array size and numbers from the user and display them on screen in the same order. The program uses pointers since the size of the array is dynamic.

```
#include <iostream>
using namespace std;

int main() {
    int total = 0;
    int *pntr;

    cout << "Enter total Number of elements";
    cin >> total;
    int arrDyn[total];
```

```
pntr = &arrDyn[0];

for (int i = 0; i < total; i++) {
    cout << endl << "Input element ";
    cin>> *pntr++;
}

pntr = &arrDyn[0];

for (int i = 0; i < total; i++) {
    cout << endl << "Element no " << i+1 << " is " << *pntr++;
}

    return 0;
}
```

Here the address of the first element of the array is assigned to the pointer pntr. Every increment increases the memory point by the size of the value it holds. So *pntr++ will take you to the next array position.

160: Write a program to create and delete an array dynamically.
Answer:

```
#include <iostream>

int main() {
    std::cout << "Enter the number of customers : ";
    int noOfCust;
```

```
std::cin >> noOfCust;

std::string *dynArry = new std::string[noOfCust]; // use array
new.
std::cout << "Allocated an array of size " << noOfCust<< '\n';

for(int i=0;i<noOfCust;i++) {
    std::cout << '\n' << "Enter customer name ";
    std::cin >> dynArry[i];
}

for(int i=0;i<noOfCust;i++) {
    std::cout << '\n' << "Customer name is " << dynArry[i];
}

delete[] dynArry; // use delete to deallocate array
return 0;
}
```

This program creates an array dynamically and deallocates the memory allocated for it after its use. The new is used to create an array and delete is used to delete it from the memory.

161: What is the difference between a string and a character array?

Answer:

Both strings and character arrays are a collection of characters which is generally used to store text like names, addresses, etc. A string always ends with a NULL value ('\0'). This is not the case

for an array of characters; the length is indicated with
strlen(string) + 1.

**162: In C, what happens if a programmer is trying to access an
array item in the index which exceeds the maximum size
assigned to the array in its declaration?**

Answer:

Since C never does bound checking, if an array is declared as size
10 then after array initialization the programmer tries to access a
12th element, the compiler will not generate an error. The
program will simply retrieve unknown, erroneous, or irrelevant
data.

163: Describe how an array variable name works in C.

Answer:

An array variable name refers to the memory address of the very
first element in the array. Its value can't be changed, so it acts like
a constant.

**164: Besides using the conventional method (array subscript), is
there another way to access array elements?**

Answer:

Array elements can also be accessed using a pointer. Since the
array name itself points to the address of the first element in the
array, by using that constant or array name, all other elements can
be accessed by using simple arithmetic operations with the array
name.

For example:

int arr[5] = [30,40,50,60,90]; # arr is an array of integers of size 5

Now to access the 3rd element using conventional method:

arr[2] #gives 50

Now to access the same value using pointer:

*(arr+2) #gives 50

165: Why are two dimensional arrays used?

Answer:

A two dimensional array is an array with a set of horizontal elements and a set of vertical elements – like a table with both rows and columns. For example, if the 2D array is storing names, the number of row elements refers to how many names can be stored in the array, while the number of column elements determines the maximum number of characters that can be used with the name information.

166: How does a programmer declare and initialize two dimensional arrays?

Answer:

Two dimensional array requires two inputs during declaration; row size and column size. There are a couple of ways to initialize a 2D array.

Syntax for declaring a 2D array:

<datatype> <2Darray_Name> [rowSize] [colSize];

Example of initializing a 2D array:

int arr_2d[2][3] = {45,23,12,67,89,54};

Or

int arr_2d[2][3] = {{45,23,12},{67,89,54}}

167: How is a 1D array passed to a function in C/C++?

Answer:

When an array is passed to a function, its starting address is passed along with the array size. To pass the address, only the array name is passed, since array name is a constant which holds the address of the first element in the array. Any changes to the array contents inside the called function reflect the same in the calling function as well. Also, in the called function the array name without its size can be declared.

168: Explain the output of the following program.

```
void main() {
    int *ptr, a[][3] = {12,32,45,67,89,90};
    ptr = a + 1;
    printf("%d", *(ptr));
    }
```

Answer:

The output will be 67, since for a two dimensional array the pointer always increments in terms of row. With one increment it will point to the starting address of the next row and a 2D array is a collection of 1D arrays.

169: Explain the output of the following program.

```
void main () {
    char arr1[] = "Hello";
    char arr2[] = "World";
    printf ("%s", arr1+arr2);
    }
```

Answer:

There will be a compiler error. The above objective can be achieved by the string concatenation library function strcat() whose prototype is declared in header file string.h.

170: Explain the output of the following program.

```
void main () {
    int X[3][2] = {{10,20},{30,40},{50,60}};
    int * ptr = X;
    printf("%d", **ptr);
    }
```

Answer:

The output will be 10 since X refers to the base address of the whole 2D array, whereas *X refers to the base address of first 1D array X[0] and **X(**ptr) refers to the first item present in the 1D array X[0].

171: Explain the output of the following program.

```
void main () {
    char arr [] = "Hello";
    arr = "World";
    printf("%s", arr);
    }
```

Answer:

The above program will throw an error saying "Lvalue required in function main" since after initializing an array it can't be reinitialized again (though the values can be modified.

172: Explain the output of the following program.

```
void main () {
    int X[3][2] = {{10,20},{30,40},{50,60}};
    printf("%d", **(X+2));
    }
```

Answer:

The output will be 50 since X carries the base address of 2D array, so X+2 will point to 3rd item of the 2D array, i.e. the third 1D array, and after dereference it will give the value as 50.

173: Explain the output of the following program.

```
void main () {
    char arr1 [] = "C prog";
    char arr2[] = "C++ Prog";
    arr1=arr2;
    printf ("%s %s", arr1,arr2) ;
    }
```

Answer:

An error will be thrown by the above program. Since an array variable is a constant (the pointer to the start of the array in memory), its value can't be changed. The above objective can be achieved by strcpy() function, whose prototype is declared in string.h.

174: Explain the output of the following program.

```
void main () {
    int X[3][2] = {{10,20},{30,40},{50,60}};
    printf("%d %d", X[1][1], *(*(X+1)+1));
```

}

Answer:

The output will be 40 40. The value of the 1st index of the output is pretty obvious, but the 2nd index of the output is also same as the first one since *(*(X+1) +1) is only another representation of X[1][1]. In the above program, (*X+1) refers to second 1D array i.e. X[1], then ((*X+1)+1) refers to the second item of the second 1D array i.e. X[1][1], but to get the value present in that index a dereference operator is used over the pointer i.e. *(*(X+1)+1)).

This page is intentionally left blank.

Chapter 13

Files in C and File Handling

175: Write a program in C to create a text file, write some text in it and then read from it.

Answer:

```
#include <iostream>
#include <fstream>
using namespace std;

int main () {
    ofstream myFileStream;
    ifstream myFileOpenStream;
    string strLine;
    myFileStream.open ("myFileTrial.txt");
    myFileStream << "Just created the file. This is my first line. \n";

    if (myFileStream.is_open()) {
```

```
        myFileStream << "Feels awesome!!! \n";
        myFileStream << "How about one more line?\n";
    }
    else cout << '\n' << "Oops!!! Can't find your file ";

    myFileStream.close();

    myFileOpenStream.open ("myFileTrial.txt");
    if (myFileOpenStream.is_open()){
        while ( getline (myFileOpenStream,strLine) ){
            cout << strLine << '\n';
        }
    }
    else cout << '\n' << "Can't find your file!!!";

    myFileOpenStream.close();
    return 0;
}
```

This program creates a file myFileTrial.txt in the system and writes 3 lines of text into it first. Then it opens the file, reads each line and prints the same.

176: What is a buffer?

Answer:

A buffer is a temporary memory which is used to hold data just before it is written into the file, printer or any other I / O device. It can be considered as the temporary repository of data while it passes between the I / O and the program. Buffer helps in holding the data temporarily when the file stream or the program is busy with something else or when there's a delay in transferring the data from the program to the file. Since it is temporary memory, as soon as the I / O device is ready to take the data, the buffer is cleared and ready for the next set of data.

177: What is a file in C?

Answer:

File refers to a location on the secondary memory (i.e. a disk). It can carry data in both binary and text format.

178: What functions are involved to access the content of a file randomly?

Answer:

For a file, the content has to be accessed randomly, not serially. There are a couple of library functions available to support this requirement such as ftell, rewind, and fseek. The function 'ftell' returns the current file pointer position in the file, "rewind" takes the file pointer position from current position to the start of the file, and "fseek" moves the file pointer position to a location desired by the programmer.

179: Explain how to open a file in C for reading or writing operations.

Answer:

Files are handled in C using a new data type pointer called FILE. The definition for the FILE pointer is declared in header file stdio.h. The programmer can use the library function fopen() to point to a particular file, and this function can create a new file in case of absence of the file or it can append to an existing file depending on the mode given as parameter to this function.

180: What is the syntax of opening and closing a file in C?
Answer:
The syntax for opening a new or existing file in C is as follows:

FILE * fopen(<const char * filename>,<const char *mode>);

In the above example, the return type of the library function 'fopen' is a FILE pointer and FILE is a new data type defined in header file stdio.h.

Syntax of closing an open file using fopen() in C is as follows:

int fclose (FILE * ptr);

In this example, the library function fclose takes the pointer of type new data type FILE which is declared in header file stfio.h.

181: What are file modes available that can be passed to the library function fopen() while opening a file in C?
Answer:
A file mode is passed as a second argument to the library function fopen() while opening a file in C. This defines the different actions taken if the file doesn't already exist in the file system as well as defining whether a file will be opened for read or write operations or an append operation. The available modes are 'r', 'r+', 'w', 'w+', 'a', 'a+'.

182: What is the difference between file modes 'r+' and 'w+' while passing them as parameters to library function fopen() for opening a file?

Answer:

Though both file modes 'r+' and 'w+' enable the FILE pointer for reading and writing operations, the main difference lies when the file path passed as the first argument to fopen() is not present in the file system. In this case, 'r+' can't create a new file in the same path, but 'w+' creates a new file in the same path if it doesn't exist.

183: How is a file opened in C++ for different operations?

Answer:

There are three classes available in C++,for reading or writing files in C, and there are two ways a file can be opened, either using constructor of those classes or the member function 'open()' of those classes. The classes are fstream, ifstream, ofstream.

This page is intentionally left blank.

Chapter 14

Exception Handling in C++

184: What is a catch-all handler?

Answer:

Catch-all handlers are used when you want to make sure that your exception handling block covers all types of exceptions known and even those unknown. It is like the usual try -catch block only. The only difference is that, instead of a known exception, the catch block uses the ellipses operator to catch an exception of any data type. The syntax is

try {

    throw <exception>;

}

catch (<datatype> <variable_name>) {

    // implement your code here

}

catch (...) { // this is catch-all handler. It will catch any other data type not mentioned above

    // implement your code here

}

It can be used to make sure that the program does not throw any exception when it encounters an unexpected and unhandled data type. If you leave the catch-all blank, the program will continue after the try section.

185: What is an exception specifier?

Answer:

An exception specifier tells the compiler whether a function intends to throw an exception and sometimes even the type of exception it may throw. The throw() function is used as the exception specifier. It can be used in 3 ways. A blank throw() without anything mentioned in the brackets means that the function will not throw any exception. A throw(<data type>) specifies the exception data type the function may throw. This does not mean that the function will throw an exception of the specified data type. It is only an indication that the function may throw an exception. A throw(...) means it can throw an exception of any datatype. Just like the catch-all handler, the ... (ellipses) functions as the throw-all handler. Please note that all compilers and languages do not handle the exception specifiers.

186: Can we use exceptions in destructors?

Answer:

Ideally, exception handling must not be done in destructors.

When a constructor does exception handling, if anything goes wrong, the object is not created. But when exception handling is done in a destructor, and it throws an exception, the destructor may have some unfinished task of freeing the memory allocated which will terminate abruptly. This will result in a lot of junk data that remain in your memory during an abrupt program termination. What you can do instead is to write into the log file if anything goes wrong.

187: Why is exception handling required in a C program?
Answer:
Without an exception handling mechanism, during the program execution if some error occurs, then the program execution is halted, even if It is a minor error and the program execution could have continued. To avoid that, an exception handling mechanism is introduced to handle errors so that program execution can be continued.

Plus, with exception handling various error messages can created and displayed that provides information about the error.

188: What is exception handling in C++?
Answer:
It is a mechanism in C++ to handle errors, but the condition is that it can handle only synchronous exceptions occurring inside a program.

189: What types of exceptions can occur during a program execution?

Answer:

There are mainly two types of exceptions:

a) synchronous exceptions

b) asynchronous exceptions

The asynchronous exception is out of the control of the programmer since they are generated by the system not by the program logic. A synchronous exception has to be handled within the program or else the program will halt.

190: Explain asynchronous exception with an example.

Answer:

Asynchronous exceptions are not due to any fault in the program code, but due to external events which are not related to the current program. Examples include interrupts during a program execution, hardware issues, etc.

191: Explain synchronous exception with an example.

Answer:

Synchronous exceptions are due to error in logic in the program code or an input given to the program, not due to any external cause. Examples are accessing an array index that is out of range and overflow of memory. These types of exceptions are taken care by C++ exception handling mechanism.

192: What are the main keywords used for handling exceptions in C++?

Answer:

There are three keywords which are associated with handling

exceptions in C++; try, throw and catch.

193: What is the use of the try block in exception handling in C++?

Answer:

This is the block where the code that might raise errors or exceptions are enclosed, so that during program execution, only this part of program code will be considered. If any exception is raised it is passed to the next catch block to handle the exceptions.

194: What is the use of 'catch' block in exception handling in C++?

Answer:

This is the handler section for exceptions. If any exceptions occur inside a try block, then throw sends them to catch block. In catch block, if there is a match found for that particular exception type, then that exception will be taken resolved.

195: What is the use of 'throw' keywords for exception handling in C++?

Answer:

When an exception or error is generated inside a try block, then there has to be some mechanism to let the exception handler section know about the error or exception was generated in try block. That is when 'throw' is used to send the exception or error to the catch block, which can handle the exception.

196: What are the sequential steps that must happen to take care

of exceptions in a program?

Answer:

First, the program code that needs to have errors resolved must be prefixed with a 'try' keyword in order to discover the reason for the error during program execution. Next the exception handler is informed that an exception of a particular type has occurred (throw). Then the exception is caught by the catch block by matching the exception type (catch). Finally, the exception is handled so the program can continue its execution.

197: How can a function be controlled so that it can throw only a certain set of exceptions?

Answer:

An 'exception specification' can be listed while declaring a function that declares what type of exceptions the function can throw. The exception specification is prefixed with a 'throw' keyword as shown in the syntax below:

Syntax:

<return_datatype> <func_name> (<arg1,<arg2, . . .>>) throw (<Excep1,<Excep2, . . >>) ;

198: How can a function be declared so that it can't throw any exceptions out of its body?

Answer:

Here a bland 'exception specification' is used so it can't throw any exceptions. The empty parameter field in the example below means no exceptions are to throw.

Syntax:

<return_type> <func_name> (<arg1,<arg2, . . .>>) throw () ;

199: What happens if a function raises an exception which is not mentioned in the 'exception specification list'?

Answer:

Suppose only Type X or Type Y exceptions are mentioned in the exception list of a function, and the program execution throws a Type Z exception. The control of the program will be transferred to a predefined function called unexpected().

200: How can the catch block be created to accept all types of exceptions (instead of just the exception types explicitly mentioned in the catch declaration).

Answer:

This can be achieved by using a special mark of three dots '…' in the argument list of catch block as in the syntax given below:

Catch (...)

{

<body of catch block>

}

201: What are the library functions available for handling exceptions which are not caught by the catch block?

Answer:

The two library functions eventually called if the catch block couldn't handle an exception are terminate() and unexpected(). The unexpected() function can call terminate() if there is no user defined function set for the unexpected() function.

202: hat is the difference between the two library functions 'terminate' and 'unexpected'?

Answer:

The terminate() function is called when there is no matching exception handler in the catch block for the exception type thrown in the try block.

The unexpected() function is called when a function should not throw a particular type exception, but the function did throw the type exception.

203: The library function terminate() eventually calls which function in the exception handling mechanism? Plus, how can a user defined function be called instead of terminate if there is no matching handler found for an exception thrown from a try block?

Answer:

The library function terminate() eventually calls the system abort() function, which terminates the program. If the programmer wants to call a user defined function instead of terminate() , then the user defined function is set through the function 'set_terminate'.

204: What is Stack unwinding?

Answer:

This is the process of destroying objects created so far, i.e. starting from try block till an exception is thrown from try block.

Whatever objects have been created until that point are destroyed by calling their destructors, provided they are automatic objects.

Chapter 15

Memory Areas

205: What are the operators new and delete for?

Answer:

The *new* operator is used in C++ to allot memory during the runtime. The *new* operator can be used with any data type. Even though the malloc() function is available in C++ to allocate memory to a data type, the new operator not only allocates memory but also creates an object which is the key aspect of C++ being an object oriented language. The *delete* operator is used to free the memory allocated using the *new* operator. These 2 operators take care of the memory allocation and garbage collection explicitly. Memory management is an important function of the programmer, when it comes to huge programs that have hundreds of variables created. Any variable or object, after its use, can be freed from the memory by using the *delete* keyword.

206: What does a destructor do to the memory?

Answer:

The destructor deletes the object. It releases the memory allocated to an object which was assigned to it by the new operator or the constructor. A destructor is an important part of Garbage Collection done by the compiler to free the memory allocated to any obsolete object. When a program is interrupted abruptly by an *exit* keyword, the destructors are automatically called and they free the memory already allocated to the object instances. Even though it is believed that destructors are automatically called every time a program exits, it may not be 100% true in all instances. It is hence, the best practice to explicitly free all memory allocations by calling the destructors.

207: Explain the output of the following program.

```
void main () {
    int i, j ;
    for (i=1,j=0; j<5; i++);
        printf("%d %d", i,j);
}
```

Answer:

There will be no Output. The program will run forever until it is cancelled or the stack overflows. Since the conditional variable j was never incremented inside the loop its value will always be 0 and always less than 5, never meeting the exit condition of the loop (j being more than or equal to 5).

208: What is the use of the stack in C program?

Answer:

Stack refers to a memory area where parameters passed by a calling function to a called function are stored, as well as return address and variables declared locally inside a function. It also carries the return address of the function. Auto variables are allocated in stack area of main memory.

209: What is the use of heap in C program?

Answer:

Heap refers to a memory area where variables created dynamically are stored. Generally, a pointer is declared to track the dynamic memory location of a variable. Apart from these, global and static variables are also created in the heap area of main memory.

210: Explain the output of the following program.

```
void main (){
    char arr[] = "Hello";
    char arr2[];
    gets(arr2);
    printf("%s %s", arr, arr2);
    }
```

Answer:

There will be a compiler error, "Size of 'arr' is unknown or zero in function main". An array size is optional when the initialization is done at the time of array declaration like : char arr[] = "Hello", but if the initialization is done after the array declaration, then the array size is mandatory for the array declaration, for example, char arr[10]; arr = "Hello";

This page is intentionally left blank.

Chapter 16

Classes and its Properties

211: What is an anonymous variable?

Answer:

For simple calculations and expressions, we need not use a variable as such and directly do the calculation or check the expression. In such cases, we do not use named variables and just use the expression or the calculation instead. We can even use them for passing on to a function. These are anonymous variables as they are not declared as named variables. Instead, the compiler takes up an anonymous memory area to calculate and returns the resultant value instead of a variable value. For example:

```
findMargin (int amount) {
    int margin = amount – 100;
    std:: cout << "Margin is " << margin << endl;
}
```

```
int main() {
    int total = 300 + 230;
    findMargin(total);

    return 0;
}
```

The above program can be rewritten as:

```
findMargin (int amount) {
    std:: cout << "Margin is " << amount – 100 << endl;
}

int main() {
    findMargin(300 + 230);

    return 0;
}
```

We have avoided allocating memory to 2 int variables and instead used anonymous variables with the expressions. If we are not going to use a variable more than once, we can use this method instead.

212: What is the difference between a protected function and a friend function?

Answer:

A friend function can access the private members of a class of which it is a friend, as if the function is also a member of the class. But a protected function can be accessed only by the sub-classes of a class. Only the inherited classes can access the protected members – functions and variables. But the friend function can access all private members of the friend class. You need to declare the function as a friend function in the class for which it is a friend. You can define the function outside the class and yet, because it is a friend, it can access all private members of the class.

213: What is an explicit constructor?

Answer:

Explicit constructors are used when you do not want the compiler to implicitly convert the datatype to a compatible one for the particular constructor. For example, if you have defined a constructor for int and float type in your program and when you try to pass a char value instead, the constructor with int type may convert the char into its number equivalent and execute. But when you specifically do not want to compiler to do that implicit conversion, declare the constructor with the keyword *explicit*. For example,

Without explicit

```
class myName {
    private:
        std:: string my_Name;
    public:
// this will work even with a char data type
    myName(int size) {
        my_Name.resize(size);
```

```
        }
}
```

With explicit
```
class myName {
    private:
        std:: string my_Name;
    public:
    // this will NOT work with any other data type
        explicit myName(int size) {
            my_Name.resize(size);
        }
}
```

214: What are virtual base classes?

Answer:

Virtual Base classes are declared when more than one class is inheriting the same base class and accessing its members. To avoid the ambiguity, C++ has introduced the keyword virtual to make sure that the compiler creates a separate copy of the base class for each derived class. There are cases when more than one class is derived based on the same class and then another class is created which is derived from these 2 derived classes. For example:

```
class base1 {
    protected:
    int valbs;
}
class A : virtual public base1 {
```

```
    protected:
    int vala;
}
class B : virtual public base1 {
    protected:
    int valb;
}
class C : public A, B{
    int valc;
}
```

Here A, B and C can access valbs. If the class base1 is not inherited as virtual class, when any of these classes access the member valbs, there's an ambiguity on its value. Once the base class is inherited as virtual, it creates a shared copy of valbs.

215: What is an interface class in C++?

Answer:

In C++, the Interface classes are classes that do not have any member variables and have only pure virtual functions. It is basically like a framework for a class and the functions are implemented when the class is interface by another class. An interface class will have details as to the functionalities expected. How they are to be implemented or how they work is defined by some other class. One classic example is a Vehicle interface. All vehicles have wheels and they run. How a bicycle runs is different from how a car runs. So the Car class will implement the interface Vehicle and also define how it runs. Similarly, the bicycle class

will also implement the vehicle interface and define how it runs.
Interface classes are used to implement multiple inheritance
where the particular language does not allow the same directly.

216: What is the output of this program?

```
#include<iostream>
class myTrialClass{
    int int1;
    public:
    myTrialClass(int abc) {
        int1 = ++abc;
    }
    void Display(){
        std::cout << '\n' << --int1 << " ";
    }
};
int main(){
    myTrialClass objTC(10);
    objTC.Display();

    int *ptr = (int*) &objTC;
    *ptr = 20;

    objTC.Display();
    return 0;
}
```

Answer:

The output is

10

19

In the first instance, when objTC.Display(); is called, the value of objTC is set to be 10. The statement myTrialClass objTC(10); creates a new object of the class myTrialClass which calls the constructor with value as 10. So the value of int1 is set as ++10 or 11. When the display() function is called, it displays --int1 which is 11 − 1 = 10, which printed on screen first. Then the pointer directly accesses the address of int1 and changes its value to 20. Then when display() function is called, --int1 is printed which is 20 − 1 which is 19.

217: What is a constructor and what is its primary function?
Answer:
A constructor is a special type of method that can be defined inside a class and this is the first method to be called while an object is created for a class. It is of two types, default constructor and parameterized constructor.
The primary function of a constructor is to initialize the data members when an object of a class is instantiated. If arguments are passed to the constructor, then it is called a parameterized constructor. If the constructor doesn't take any parameters, then it is called a default constructor. Also, another type of constructor is the dummy constructor, which is not defined inside the class. It is the responsibility of the complier to call a dummy constructor.

218: What is class in C++?
Answer:

Class is a type of data structure for creating user defined data types and it contains not only data but also functions. Both data and functions can be coupled together inside a class and an object can be created which will have its own instance of data members, but functions remain shared for all the objects of a single class. Class only presents the skeleton of a user defined data type; it doesn't implement those data members. To implement the data members present inside the class, a programmer needs to create the object of the class (i.e. instantiation of class).

219: What is the difference between constructor and destructor in C++?

Answer:

Constructor is a special member function which is called every time a class is instantiated and this is the first member function. It is called before any other member function can be called by the program.

Destructor is also a special member function called when an object goes out of scope in case of local object variables defined in a function, but for global object variables, the destructor is called just before the program is going to be finished.

Constructor can be overloaded, but destructor can't be overloaded, since destructor can't take any argument and can't return any value. So a class contains only one destructor.

220: What is inheritance and what are the different types of inheritance?

Answer:

Inheritance is a property of Object Oriented programming where a new class is derived from another class, thus creating a hierarchical relationship. Also, inheritance is used to avoid writing the same logic already defined in one of the parent class member functions. The derived class is called child class and the parent class is where the child class is derived.

The various types of inheritance are: single, multilevel, multiple, hierarchical, hybrid and multipath inheritance.

221: What is copy constructor?

Answer:

A constructor of a class can accept parameters and those constructors are called parameterized constructors. If a constructor accepts its own object as parameter, then that constructor is called copy constructor.

222: What is friend function and how is it declared?

Answer:

This special function is declared with a prefix 'friend' and it allows nonmember functions to access the private members of a class indirectly using objects. When the friend function is declared inside a class, then only the prefix 'friend' is used, but when the logic is defined for the function outside the class, then it doesn't use the prefix 'friend'.

223: Where friend function can be used in C++?

Answer:

The friend function can be used while overloading operators.

Also, if the programmer wants to operate on two different class objects at a time, it is very convenience to use a friend function.

224: What is Single heritance, explain with diagram.

Answer:

Single heritance is a form of inheritance where the child class is derived from only a single base class. Here a child class can have at most one parent class, and the parent class can also have at most one child class.

Parent_Class_A <<-- Child_Class_B

225: What is Multiple inheritance and how does it differ from Hierarchical inheritance?

Answer:

Multiple inheritance is a form of inheritance where a child class is derived from more than one base class; for example a child class can have more than one parent class. But in case of Hierarchical inheritance, more than one child class is derived from a single parent class. Therefore Multiple and Hierarchical are the two opposite forms of inheritance.

226: What is Multilevel inheritance and how does it differ from Single inheritance?

Answer:

Multilevel inheritance exists when one child class is derived from another child class, i.e., a child class has become child of another child class. In this way, the chain of derived classes can be more, but in single inheritance there is only a single derived class.

227: What is polymorphism in C++? Name the types of polymorphism.

Answer:

Polymorphism is one of the objectives of object oriented programming. It allows one function name to be used for different purposes. There are three different types of ways to achieve polymorphism:

   a) Function overloading
   b) Operator overloading
   c) Dynamic binding

228: What is a data member and a member function inside a class?

Answer:

A data member represents data inside a class. To manipulate the data of an object, member functions are declared inside a class, so that an object calls a member function of a class, and then implements the data members and their values to perform operations.

229: What is an object in C++?

Answer:

An object is an instance of a class. Once the class is declared, it means a structure or blueprint of a particular user defined data type is mentioned. To manipulate those data members present inside a class, an object is declared and the object accesses and modifies the data members using member functions present inside the class.

230: How is an object of a class created and how are the members of a class using object accessed?

Answer:

An object of a class can be created by using the following syntax:

class <class_name> <Objec_name1>,<object_name2>, . . .

In the above example the 'class' keyword is not mandatory while instantiating a class.

Object can access members of a class by using 'member access operator'. The syntax is given below:

<object_name> . <member_of_class> ['.' Is the member access operator]

231: What is an inline member function in C++?

Answer:

When member functions are defined inside a class, then they become inline member functions. Also the member functions defined outside the class can be made inline by prefixing the word 'inline'. Inline member functions have an advantage over normal functions in the way that the caller is replaced with the function itself, thus reducing the overhead of transferring controls through a function call and return.

232: When can inline member function be used?

Answer:

If the function contains very few statements, then instead of calling the function It is better to replace the function itself to the caller. The execution time for the inline member function is less than the time required to call a function and return from it. Since the compiler replaces the code for the inline member function, it is mandatory to let the compiler know all the instructions present in the function properly.

233: What are static data members for a class and how they are declared and initialized?

Answer:

Static data members for a class are like static variables in C. Static data members for a class remains active across all the objects of a class, i.e. the value carried by the static data member for a previous object can be seen by the current object. It can be declared using 'static' keyword as a prefix.

        static <datatype> <dataMember_name>;

Also, since the value for a static data member remains valid across all the objects, so the definition of a static data member is done outside the class as mentioned below:

        <datatype> <name_of_the_class> :: <dataMember_name> = <value>

234: When do static members can come in handy while coding in C++?

Answer:

When the programmer wants to keep track of a variable for all the objects of a class (like calculating how many objects are still alive or how many total objects have been created so far), it is accomplished by implementing static members for a class.

235: What is the difference between class and structure?

Answer:

With structure, the default access specifier is 'public' (i.e. if no access specifier is declared explicitly) the compiler takes the data members as public, where as in class the default access specifier is 'private'.

236: What is dynamic object in C++?

Answer:

Like dynamic memory allocation for data variables at run time, a class can also be initialized or instantiated at run time by using the 'new' operator and those objects are called 'dynamic objects'. Like dynamic memory allocation for normal data variables, dynamic objects also allocate memory from heap.

237: What are the different access control specifiers that can be used while declaring a class?

Answer:

There are three access control specifiers, public, private, and protected, that can be used while declaring a class - depending on the security. The default access control specifier is private. When members of the class are declared using private, then they can only be accessed by the class members, not by the objects. In case of public, the members can be accesses by both class members as well as objects. The protected class specifier is used while implementing inheritance so data members can be accessed by class members as well as members of the child class.

238: What is 'this' pointer?

Answer:

A 'this' pointer is a special pointer declared automatically inside very member functions of a class. And the pointer holds the address of the class object to which the member function is pointing to.

239: What are nameless objects?

Answer:

Nameless objects are a class that gets destroyed instantly after the statement declaring them is executed. The scope of these objects is not beyond the statement which declares them. The syntax is given below:

<classname> (<argument1,argument2,...>);

240: What is constructor overloading in C++?

Answer:

A class can have a member function whose name matches the name of the class itself, and that member function is called constructor. A class can have more than one such function that differs only in terms of their signature, i.e. types of arguments accepted by those functions or number of arguments being accepted by them or both.

241: What are default and parameterized constructors?

Answer:

When defining a constructor it can accept arguments as well. So, depending upon whether arguments can be accepted by the constructor, it is of two types: default and parameterized constructors. If arguments are passed to the constructor, then it called parameterized constructor .If a constructor doesn't take any parameters, then it is called default constructor.

242: What are the limitations of static member functions of a class?

Answer:

Static member functions in a class can only access static data members declared in the same class. They can't access non-static data members declared in that class. However, static member functions can be accessed without using class object provided the static member function is declared as public.

243: What are empty classes?

Answer:

It is possible to declare classes without having any data members or member functions. These classes without code are called empty classes. They are generally used in checking the exception handling mechanisms employed while developing a project involving object oriented methodologies.

244: What is encapsulation?

Answer:

An encapsulation is an object oriented mechanism by which data and functions are bounded together as a single unit. Typically, data is declared inside the private of a class and only the member functions can manipulate that data.

245: How is the data hiding mechanism achieved in C++?
Answer:

Data hiding is achieved using the class specifier 'private'.
Generally data members are declared as private and the member
functions which act on those data are defined as public. In this
way, the data is only available to member functions and not to any
other functions outside the class - thus hiding the data from
others.

246: What is a pure virtual function?
Answer:

Sometimes virtual functions are defined in the base class without
any code inside them, and are therefore called pure virtual
functions. Since this function doesn't implement coding, this
function is overridden in the child classes.

247: What are abstract and concrete classes?
Answer:

Classes whose objects can't be created or the classes which can't be
instantiated are called abstract classes. Those classes contain pure
virtual functions thus their objects cannot be declared. The classes
which can be instantiated are called concrete classes.

248: What points should a programmer remember while creating virtual functions?
Answer:

The prototype of the virtual function in both parent and child
class must be same. Virtual functions should be created in the

public part of a class. Virtual functions are not static member functions.

249: What are live objects in C++?

Answer:

Like other standard data types such as int and char, class objects can also be created dynamically. These objects created dynamically are called live objects. This is achieved by using a new operator which is available for allocating memory dynamically. The syntax of creating such objects is shown below:

```
<class_name> * <Ptr_name> = new <class_name>
(<argument1,<argument2, ...>>)
```

250: How are virtual functions defined and why are they used?

Answer:

Virtual functions are declared using the keyword 'virtual' as a prefix, and they are declared in the base class. To achieve the concept of function overriding and dynamic binding, virtual functions are used. The syntax of declaring a virtual function is shown below:

```
virtual <returnDatatype> <Name_of_function>
(<arg1,<arg2,..>>)
```

HR Questions

Review these typical interview questions and think about how you would answer them. Read the answers listed; you will find best possible answers along with strategies and suggestions.

1: Where do you find ideas?

Answer:

Ideas can come from all places, and an interviewer wants to see that your ideas are just as varied. Mention multiple places that you gain ideas from, or settings in which you find yourself brainstorming. Additionally, elaborate on how you record ideas or expand upon them later.

2: How do you achieve creativity in the workplace?

Answer:

It's important to show the interviewer that you're capable of being resourceful and innovative in the workplace, without stepping outside the lines of company values. Explain where ideas normally stem from for you (examples may include an exercise such as list-making or a mind map), and connect this to a particular task in your job that it would be helpful to be creative in.

3: How do you push others to create ideas?

Answer:

If you're in a supervisory position, this may be requiring employees to submit a particular number of ideas, or to complete regular idea-generating exercises, in order to work their creative muscles. However, you can also push others around you to create ideas simply by creating more of your own. Additionally, discuss with the interviewer the importance of questioning people as a way to inspire ideas and change.

4: Describe your creativity.

Answer:

Try to keep this answer within the professional realm, but if you have an impressive background in something creative outside of your employment history, don't be afraid to include it in your answer also. The best answers about creativity will relate problem-solving skills, goal-setting, and finding innovative ways to tackle a project or make a sale in the workplace. However, passions outside of the office are great, too (so long as they don't cut into your work time or mental space).

5: How would you handle a negative coworker?

Answer:

Everyone has to deal with negative coworkers – and the single best way to do so is to remain positive. You may try to build a relationship with the coworker or relate to them in some way, but even if your efforts are met with a cold shoulder, you must retain your positive attitude. Above all, stress that you would never allow a coworker's negativity to impact your own work or productivity.

6: What would you do if you witnessed a coworker surfing the web, reading a book, etc, wasting company time?

Answer:

The interviewer will want to see that you realize how detrimental it is for employees to waste company time, and that it is not something you take lightly. Explain the way you would adhere to company policy, whether that includes talking to the coworker yourself, reporting the behavior straight to a supervisor, or talking to someone in HR.

7: How do you handle competition among yourself and other employees?

Answer:

Healthy competition can be a great thing, and it is best to stay focused on the positive aspects of this here. Don't bring up conflict among yourself and other coworkers, and instead focus on the motivation to keep up with the great work of others, and the ways in which coworkers may be a great support network in helping to push you to new successes.

8: When is it okay to socialize with coworkers?

Answer:

This question has two extreme answers (all the time, or never), and your interviewer, in most cases, will want to see that you fall somewhere in the middle. It's important to establish solid relationships with your coworkers, but never at the expense of getting work done. Ideally, relationship-building can happen with exercises of teamwork and special projects, as well as in the break room.

9: Tell me about a time when a major change was made at your last job, and how you handled it.

Answer:

Provide a set-up for the situation including the old system, what the change was, how it was implemented, and the results of the change, and include how you felt about each step of the way. Be sure that your initial thoughts on the old system are neutral, and that your excitement level grows with each step of the new change, as an interviewer will be pleased to see your adaptability.

10: When delegating tasks, how do you choose which tasks go to which team members?

Answer:

The interviewer is looking to gain insight into your thought process with this question, so be sure to offer thorough reasoning behind your choice. Explain that you delegate tasks based on each individual's personal strengths, or that you look at how many other projects each person is working on at the time, in order to create the best fit possible.

11: Tell me about a time when you had to stand up for something you believed strongly about to coworkers or a supervisor.

Answer:

While it may be difficult to explain a situation of conflict to an interviewer, this is a great opportunity to display your passions and convictions, and your dedication to your beliefs. Explain not just the situation to the interviewer, but also elaborate on why it was so important to you to stand up for the issue, and how your coworker or supervisor responded to you afterward – were they more respectful? Unreceptive? Open-minded? Apologetic?

12: Tell me about a time when you helped someone finish their

work, even though it wasn't "your job."

Answer:

Though you may be frustrated when required to pick up someone else's slack, it's important that you remain positive about lending a hand. The interviewer will be looking to see if you're a team player, and by helping someone else finish a task that he or she couldn't manage alone, you show both your willingness to help the team succeed, and your own competence.

13 What are the challenges of working on a team? How do you handle this?

Answer:

There are many obvious challenges to working on a team, such as handling different perspectives, navigating individual schedules, or accommodating difficult workers. It's best to focus on one challenge, such as individual team members missing deadlines or failing to keep commitments, and then offer a solution that clearly addresses the problem. For example, you could organize weekly status meetings for your team to discuss progress, or assign shorter deadlines in order to keep the long-term deadline on schedule.

14: Do you value diversity in the workplace?

Answer:

Diversity is important in the workplace in order to foster an environment that is accepting, equalizing, and full of different perspectives and backgrounds. Be sure to show your awareness of these issues, and stress the importance of learning from others' experiences.

15: How would you handle a situation in which a coworker was not accepting of someone else's diversity?

Answer:

Explain that it is important to adhere to company policies regarding diversity, and that you would talk to the relevant supervisors or management team. When it is appropriate, it could also be best to talk to the coworker in question about the benefits of alternate perspectives – if you can handle the situation yourself, it's best not to bring resolvable issues to management.

16: Are you rewarded more from working on a team, or accomplishing a task on your own?

Answer:

It's best to show a balance between these two aspects – your employer wants to see that you're comfortable working on your own, and that you can complete tasks efficiently and well without assistance. However, it's also important for your employer to see that you can be a team player, and that you understand the value that multiple perspectives and efforts can bring to a project.

17: Tell me about a time when you didn't meet a deadline.

Answer:

Ideally, this hasn't happened – but if it has, make sure you use a minor example to illustrate the situation, emphasize how long ago it happened, and be sure that you did as much as you could to ensure that the deadline was met. Additionally, be sure to include what you learned about managing time better or prioritizing tasks in order to meet all future deadlines.

18: How do you eliminate distractions while working?

Answer:

With the increase of technology and the ease of communication, new distractions arise every day. Your interviewer will want to see that you are still able to focus on work, and that your productivity has not been affected, by an example showing a routine you employ in order to stay on task.

19: Tell me about a time when you worked in a position with a weekly or monthly quota to meet. How often were you successful?

Answer:

Your numbers will speak for themselves, and you must answer this question honestly. If you were regularly met your quotas, be sure to highlight this in a confident manner and don't be shy in pointing out your strengths in this area. If your statistics are less than stellar, try to point out trends in which they increased toward the end of your employment, and show reflection as to ways you can improve in the future.

20: Tell me about a time when you met a tough deadline, and how you were able to complete it.

Answer:

Explain how you were able to prioritize tasks, or to delegate portions of an assignments to other team members, in order to deal with a tough deadline. It may be beneficial to specify why the deadline was tough – make sure it's clear that it was not a result of procrastination on your part. Finally, explain how you were able to successfully meet the deadline, and what it took to get there in the end.

21: How do you stay organized when you have multiple projects on your plate?

Answer:

The interviewer will be looking to see that you can manage your time and work well – and being able to handle multiple projects at once, and still giving each the attention it deserves, is a great mark of a worker's competence and efficiency. Go through a typical process of goal-setting and prioritizing, and explain the steps of these to the interviewer, so he or she can see how well you manage time.

22: How much time during your work day do you spend on "auto-pilot?"

Answer:

While you may wonder if the employer is looking to see how efficient you are with this question (for example, so good at your job that you don't have to think about it), but in almost every case, the employer wants to see that you're constantly thinking, analyzing, and processing what's going on in the workplace. Even if things are running smoothly, there's usually an opportunity somewhere to make things more efficient or to increase sales or productivity. Stress your dedication to ongoing development, and convey that being on "auto-pilot" is not conducive to that type of success.

23: How do you handle deadlines?

Answer:

The most important part of handling tough deadlines is to prioritize tasks and set goals for completion, as well as to delegate or eliminate unnecessary work. Lead the interviewer through a general scenario, and display your competency through your ability to organize and set priorities, and most importantly, remain calm.

24: Tell me about your personal problem-solving process.

Answer:

Your personal problem-solving process should include outlining the problem, coming up with possible ways to fix the problem, and setting a clear action plan that leads to resolution. Keep your answer brief and organized, and explain the steps in a concise, calm manner that shows you are level-headed even under stress.

25: What sort of things at work can make you stressed?

Answer:

As it's best to stay away from negatives, keep this answer brief and simple. While answering that nothing at work makes you stressed will not be very believable to the interviewer, keep your answer to one generic principle such as when members of a team don't keep their commitments, and then focus on a solution you generally employ to tackle that stress, such as having weekly status meetings or intermittent deadlines along the course of a project.

26: What do you look like when you are stressed about something? How do you solve it?

Answer:

This is a trick question – your interviewer wants to hear that you don't look any different when you're stressed, and that you don't allow negative emotions to interfere with your productivity. As far as how you solve your stress, it's best if you have a simple solution mastered, such as simply taking deep breaths and counting to 10 to bring yourself back to the task at hand.

27: Can you multi-task?

Answer:

Some people can, and some people can't. The most important part of multi-tasking is to keep a clear head at all times about what needs to be done, and what priority each task falls under. Explain how you evaluate tasks to determine priority, and how you manage your time in order to ensure that all are completed efficiently.

28: How many hours per week do you work?

Answer:

Many people get tricked by this question, thinking that answering more hours is better – however, this may cause an employer to wonder why you have to work so many hours in order to get the work done that other people can do in a shorter amount of time.

Give a fair estimate of hours that it should take you to complete a job, and explain that you are also willing to work extra whenever needed.

29: How many times per day do you check your email?
Answer:

While an employer wants to see that you are plugged into modern technology, it is also important that the number of times you check your email per day is relatively low – perhaps two to three times per day (dependent on the specific field you're in). Checking email is often a great distraction in the workplace, and while it is important to remain connected, much correspondence can simply be handled together in the morning and afternoon.

30: How do you make decisions?
Answer:

This is a great opportunity for you to wow your interviewer with your decisiveness, confidence, and organizational skills. Make sure that you outline a process for decision-making, and that you stress the importance of weighing your options, as well as in trusting intuition. If you answer this question skillfully and with ease, your interviewer will trust in your capability as a worker.

31: What are the most difficult decisions for you to make?
Answer:

Explain your relationship to decision-making, and a general synopsis of the process you take in making choices. If there is a particular type of decision that you often struggle with, such as those that involve other people, make sure to explain why that type of decision is tough for you, and how you are currently engaged in improving your skills.

32: When making a tough decision, how do you gather information?

Answer:

If you're making a tough choice, it's best to gather information from as many sources as possible. Lead the interviewer through your process of taking information from people in different areas, starting first with advice from experts in your field, feedback from coworkers or other clients, and by looking analytically at your own past experiences.

33: Tell me about a decision you made that did not turn out well.

Answer:

Honesty and transparency are great values that your interviewer will appreciate – outline the choice you made, why you made it, the results of your poor decision – and finally (and most importantly!) what you learned from the decision. Give the interviewer reason to trust that you wouldn't make a decision like that again in the future.

34: Are you able to make decisions quickly?

Answer:

You may be able to make decisions quickly, but be sure to communicate your skill in making sound, thorough decisions as well. Discuss the importance of making a decision quickly, and how you do so, as well as the necessity for each decision to first be well-informed

35: What is the best way for a company to advertise?

Answer:

If you're going for a position in any career other than marketing, this question is probably intended to demonstrate your ability to think critically and to provide reflective support for your answers. As such, the particular method you choose is not so important as why you've chosen it. For example, word of mouth advertising is important because customers will inherently trust the source, and social media advertising is important as it reaches new customers quickly and cheaply.

36: Is it better to gain a new customer or to keep an old one?

Answer:

In almost every case, it is better to keep an old customer, and it's important that you are able to articulate why this is. First, new customers generally cost companies more than retaining old ones does, and new customers are more likely to switch to a different company. Additionally, keeping old customers is a great way to provide a stable backbone for the company, as well as to also gain new customers as they are likely to recommend your company to friends.

37: What is the best way to win clients from competitors?

Answer:

There are many schools of thought on the best way to win clients from competitors, and unless you know that your interviewer adheres to a specific thought or practice, it's best to keep this question general. Rather than using absolute language, focus on the benefits of one or two strategies and show a clear, critical understanding of how these ways can succeed in a practical application.

38: How do you feel about companies monitoring internet usage?

Answer:

Generally speaking, most companies will monitor some degree of internet usage over their employees – and during an interview is not the best time to rebel against this practice. Instead, focus on positive aspects such as the way it can lead to increased productivity for some employees who may be easily lost in the world of resourceful information available to them.

39: What is your first impression of our company?

Answer:

Obviously, this should be a positive answer! Pick out a couple key components of the company's message or goals that you especially identify with or that pertain to your experience, and discuss why you believe these missions are so important.

40: Tell me about your personal philosophy on business.

Answer:

Your personal philosophy on business should be well-thought out, and in line with the missions and objectives of the company.

Stay focused on positive aspects such as the service it can provide, and the lessons people gain in business, and offer insight as to where your philosophy has come from.

41: What's most important in a business model: sales, customer service, marketing, management, etc.?

Answer:

For many positions, it may be a good strategy to tailor this answer to the type of field you're working in, and to explain why that aspect of business is key. However, by explaining that each aspect is integral to the function as a whole, you can display a greater sense of business savvy to the interviewer and may stand out in his or her mind as a particularly aware candidate.

42: How do you keep up with news and emerging trends in the field?

Answer:

The interviewer wants to see that you are aware of what's currently going on in your field. It is important that your education does not stop after college, and the most successful candidates will have a list of resources they regularly turn to already in place, so that they may stay aware and engaged in developing trends.

43: Would you have a problem adhering to company policies on social media?

Answer:

Social media concerns in the workplace have become a greater issue, and many companies now outline policies for the use of social media. Interviewers will want to be assured that you won't have a problem adhering to company standards, and that you will maintain a consistent, professional image both in the office and online.

44: Tell me about one of the greatest problems facing X industry today.

Answer:

If you're involved in your career field, and spend time on your own studying trends and new developments, you should be able to display an awareness of both problems and potential solutions coming up in the industry. Research some of the latest news before heading into the interview, and be prepared to discuss current events thoroughly.

45: What do you think it takes to be successful in our company?

Answer:

Research the company prior to the interview. Be aware of the company's mission and main objectives, as well as some of the biggest names in the company, and also keep in mind how they achieved success. Keep your answer focused on specific objectives you could reach in order to help the company achieve its goals.

46: What is your favorite part of working in this career field?

Answer:

This question is an opportunity to discuss some of your favorite aspects of the job, and to highlight why you are a great candidate for the particular position. Choose elements of the work you enjoy that are related to what you would do if hired for the position. Remember to remain enthusiastic and excited for the opportunities you could attain in the job.

47: What do you see happening to your career in the next 10 years?

Answer:

If you're plugged in to what's happening in your career now, and are making an effort to stay abreast of emerging trends in your field, you should be able to offer the interviewer several predictions as to where your career or field may be heading. This insight and level of awareness shows a level of dedication and interest that is important to employers.

48: What are the three most important things you're looking for in a position?

Answer:

The top three things you want in a position should be similar to the top three things the employer wants from an employee, so that it is clear that you are well-matched to the job. For example, the employer wants a candidate who is well-qualified for and has practical experience – and you want a position that allows you to use your education and skills to their best applications. The employer wants a candidate who is willing to take on new challenges and develop new systems to increase sales or productivity – and you want a position that pushes you and offers opportunities to develop, create, and lead new initiatives. The employer wants a candidate who will grow into and stay with the company for a long time – and you want a position that offers stability and believes in building a strong team. Research what the employer is looking for beforehand, and match your objectives to theirs.

49: How are you evaluating the companies you're looking to work with?

Answer:

While you may feel uncomfortable exerting your own requirements during the interview, the employer wants to see that you are thinking critically about the companies you're applying with, just as they are critically looking at you. Don't be afraid to specify what your needs from a company are (but do try to make sure they match up well with the company – preferably before you apply there), and show confidence and decisiveness in your answer. The interviewer wants to know that you're the kind of person who knows what they want, and how to get it.

50: Are you comfortable working for _____ salary?

Answer:

If the answer to this question is no, it may be a bit of a deal-breaker in a first interview, as you are unlikely to have much room to negotiate. You can try to leverage a bit by highlighting specific experience you have, and how that makes you qualified for more, but be aware that this is very difficult to navigate at this step of the process. To avoid this situation, be aware of industry standards and, if possible, company standards, prior to your application.

51: Why did you choose your last job?
Answer:

In learning what led you to your last job, the interviewer is able to get a feel for the types of things that motivate you. Keep these professionally-focused, and remain passionate about the early points of your career, and how excited you were to get started in the field.

52: How long has it been since your last job and why?
Answer:

Be sure to have an explanation prepared for all gaps in employment, and make sure it's a professional reason. Don't mention difficulties you may have had in finding a job, and instead focus on positive things such as pursuing outside interests or perhaps returning to school for additional education.

53: What other types of jobs have you been looking for?
Answer:

The answer to this question can show the interviewer that you're both on the market and in demand. Mention jobs you've applied for or looked at that are closely related to your field, or similar to the position you're interviewing for. Don't bring up last-ditch efforts that found you applying for a part-time job completely unrelated to your field.

54: Have you ever been disciplined at work?

Answer:

Hopefully the answer here is no – but if you have been disciplined for something at work though, be absolutely sure that you can explain it thoroughly. Detail what you learned from the situation, and reflect on how you grew after the process.

55: What is your availability like?

Answer:

Your availability should obviously be as open as possible, and any gaps in availability should be explained and accounted for. Avoid asking about vacation or personal days (as well as other benefits), and convey to the interviewer how serious you are about your work.

56: May I contact your current employer?

Answer:

If possible, it is best to allow an interviewer to contact your current employer as a reference. However, if it's important that your employer is not contacted, explain your reason tactfully, such as you just started job searching and you haven't had the opportunity yet to inform them that you are looking for other employment. Be careful of this reasoning though, as employers may wonder if you'll start shopping for something better while employed with them as well.

57: Do you have any valuable contacts you could bring to our business?

Answer:

It's great if you can bring knowledge, references, or other contacts that your new employer may be able to network with. However, be sure that you aren't offering up any of your previous employer's clients, or in any way violating contractual agreements.

58: How soon would you be available to start working?

Answer:

While you want to be sure that you're available to start as soon as possible if the company is interested in hiring you, if you still have another job, be sure to give them at least two weeks' notice. Though your new employer may be anxious for you to start, they will want to hire a worker whom they can respect for giving adequate notice, so that they won't have to worry if you'll eventually leave them in the lurch.

59: Why would your last employer say that you left?

Answer:

The key to this question is that your employer's answer must be the same as your own answer about why you left. For instance, if you've told your employer that you left to find a position with greater opportunities for career advancement, your employer had better not say that you were let go for missing too many days of work. Honesty is key in your job application process.

60: How long have you been actively looking for a job?

Answer:

It's best if you haven't been actively looking for a job for very long, as a long period of time may make the interviewer wonder why no one else has hired you. If it has been awhile, make sure to explain why, and keep it positive. Perhaps you haven't come across many opportunities that provide you with enough of a challenge or that are adequately matched to someone of your education and experience.

61: When don't you show up to work?

Answer:

Clearly, the only time acceptable to miss work is for a real emergency or when you're truly sick – so don't start bringing up times now that you plan to miss work due to vacations or family birthdays. Alternatively, you can tell the interviewer how dedicated to your work you are, and how you always strive to be fully present and to put in the same amount of work every time you come in, even when you're feeling slightly under the weather.

62: What is the most common reason you miss work?

Answer:

If there is a reason that you will miss work routinely, this is the time to disclose it – but doing so during an interview will reflect negatively on you. Ideally, you will only miss work during cases of extreme illness or other emergencies.

63: What is your attendance record like?

Answer:

Be sure to answer this question honestly, but ideally you will have already put in the work to back up the fact that you rarely miss days or arrive late. However, if there are gaps in your attendance, explain them briefly with appropriate reasons, and make sure to emphasize your dedication to your work, and reliability.

64: Where did you hear about this position?
Answer:

This may seem like a simple question, but the answer can actually speak volumes about you. If you were referred by a friend or another employee who works for the company, this is a great chance to mention your connection (if the person is in good standing!). However, if you heard about it from somewhere like a career fair or a work placement agency, you may want to focus on how pleased you were to come across such a wonderful opportunity.

65: Tell me anything else you'd like me to know when making a hiring decision.
Answer:

This is a great opportunity for you to give a final sell of yourself to the interviewer – use this time to remind the interviewer of why you are qualified for the position, and what you can bring to the company that no one else can. Express your excitement for the opportunity to work with a company pursuing X mission.

66: Why would your skills be a good match with X objective of our company?
Answer:

If you've researched the company before the interview, answering this question should be no problem. Determine several of the company's main objectives, and explain how specific skills that you have are conducive to them. Also, think about ways that your experience and skills can translate to helping the company expand upon these objectives, and to reach further goals. If your old company had a similar objective, give a specific example of how you helped the company to meet it.

67: What do you think this job entails?

Answer:

Make sure you've researched the position well before heading into the interview. Read any and all job descriptions you can find (at best, directly from the employer's website or job posting), and make note of key duties, responsibilities, and experience required. Few things are less impressive to an interviewer than a candidate who has no idea what sort of job they're actually being interviewed for.

68: Is there anything else about the job or company you'd like to know?

Answer:

If you have learned about the company beforehand, this is a great opportunity to show that you put in the effort to study before the interview. Ask questions about the company's mission in relation to current industry trends, and engage the interviewer in interesting, relevant conversation. Additionally, clear up anything else you need to know about the specific position before leaving – so that if the interviewer calls with an offer, you'll be prepared to answer.

69: Are you the best candidate for this position?
Answer:

Yes! Offer specific details about what makes you qualified for this position, and be sure to discuss (and show) your unbridled passion and enthusiasm for the new opportunity, the job, and the company.

70: How did you prepare for this interview?
Answer:

The key part of this question is to make sure that you have prepared! Be sure that you've researched the company, their objectives, and their services prior to the interview, and know as much about the specific position as you possibly can. It's also helpful to learn about the company's history and key players in the current organization.

71: If you were hired here, what would you do on your first day?
Answer:

While many people will answer this question in a boring fashion, going through the standard first day procedures, this question is actually a great chance for you to show the interviewer why you will make a great hire. In addition to things like going through training or orientation, emphasize how much you would enjoy meeting your supervisors and coworkers, or how you would spend a lot of the day asking questions and taking in all of your new surroundings.

72: Have you viewed our company's website?

Answer:

Clearly, you should have viewed the company's website and done some preliminary research on them before coming to the interview. If for some reason you did not, do not say that you did, as the interviewer may reveal you by asking a specific question about it. If you did look at the company's website, this is an appropriate time to bring up something you saw there that was of particular interest to you, or a value that you especially supported.

73: How does X experience on your resume relate to this position?

Answer:

Many applicants will have some bit of experience on their resume that does not clearly translate to the specific job in question. However, be prepared to be asked about this type of seemingly-irrelevant experience, and have a response prepared that takes into account similar skill sets or training that the two may share.

74: Why do you want this position?

Answer:

Keep this answer focused positively on aspects of this specific job that will allow you to further your skills, offer new experience, or that will be an opportunity for you to do something that you particularly enjoy. Don't tell the interviewer that you've been looking for a job for a long time, or that the pay is very appealing, or you will appear unmotivated and opportunistic.

75: How is your background relevant to this position?
Answer:

Ideally, this should be obvious from your resume. However, in instances where your experience is more loosely-related to the position, make sure that you've researched the job and company well before the interview. That way, you can intelligently relate the experience and skills that you do have, to similar skills that would be needed in the new position. Explain specifically how your skills will translate, and use words to describe your background such as "preparation" and "learning." Your prospective position should be described as an "opportunity" and a chance for "growth and development."

76: How do you feel about X mission of our company?
Answer:

It's important to have researched the company prior to the interview – and if you've done so, this question won't catch you off guard. The best answer is one that is simple, to the point, and shows knowledge of the mission at hand. Offer a few short statements as to why you believe in the mission's importance, and note that you would be interested in the chance to work with a company that supports it.

INDEX

C and C++ Interview Questions

19: Explain the output of the following program.

20: How are pointers to a structure declared? How are members of a structure accessed using this pointer?

21: What is a self-referential structure? Explain with an example.

Functions or Methods

22: What are the different types of functions based on how they are declared?

23: Explain the scope rules of functions.

24: Explain the arguments to the main () function in C++.

25: What is a void function in C++?

26: What is function overloading in C++ and how does it differ from function overriding?

27: What is a default argument while declaring a function or calling a function?

28: Why are functions used?

29: What is main() function in C and the syntax of the main function?

30: What is the difference the way function prototypes are declared in C and C++?

31: What is the difference between parameters passed by value and by pointers?

32: What is a function and how does it help programmers in developing programs?

33: How to call a function defined in a module?

34: What is the difference between actual and formal parameters?

35: What is static binding and dynamic binding?

36: How to return a value from a function?

37: What are library functions in C?

38: What is a user defined function?

39: What is the syntax of a function definition?

40: Explain the output of the below program.

41: What is the difference between pass by reference and pass by pointer while calling a function?

Recursion

42: Write a program to print the Fibonacci series using recursive function.

43: What is the output? Explain.

44: Explain some of the functionalities that can be processed using recursion.

45: What is recursion in C?

46: What are advantages and disadvantages of using recursion?

Pointer and its Handling

47: Explain pointer variables and pointer operators in C++.

48: Explain Multiple Indirection in C++.

49: What are the common errors committed while using pointers?

50: Explain these pointer declarations.

51: What is a pointer in C and when a pointer can be referred as a wild pointer?

52: What is a void pointer?

53: What is a NULL pointer?

54: What is an array of pointers and how it is declared?

55: What is a constant pointer and how is it declared?

56: How is the pointer to a constant variable declared?

57: Where can near and far pointers be used?

58: What is the syntax for declaring a far pointer?

59: Explain, using an example, how constant pointer and pointer to constant variable are different.

60: How is constant pointer declared so it doesn't allow the variable's content or value to be changed?

61: Explain the output of the following program.

62: Explain the output of the following program.

63: Explain the output of the following program.

64: How is a pointer defined to a function and how is function called using the pointer variable?

65: What is dangling reference in C and when is it a factor?

66: What is garbage memory and when does it come into picture?

67: In terms of the pointer, what is indirection or dereference operator?

68: What is the address operator in relation to the pointer in C?

69: What will be the value of the following program and explain why.

70: Explain the output of the following program.

71: Explain the output of the following program.

Templates

72: What is a template in C++?

73: Why do we need templates in C++?

74: What is the syntax of declaring a function template?

75: What is the syntax for declaring a class template?

General Concepts

76: What are the three basic concepts of C++?

77: Explain Preprocessing in C++.

78: What are the different ways in which the static keyword is used?

79: Have a look at the following program. Explain whether it will compile and execute in both C & C++.

80: What is source code and object code in C?

81: What are command line arguments?

82: What is the use of header file in C? Use the example of stdio.h to explain a header file.

83: What is the difference if a header file is included in C in the following two ways?

84: What is the role of linker in C?

85: What is the maximum value for a 16 bit integer in both signed and

109: What is the scope of a variable?

110: What is the difference between the way variables are defined in C and C++?

111: What is operator overloading and how it can be achieved?

112: Where can the scope resolution operator be used in C++?

113: How unary and binary operators are different in C?

114: What is ternary operator and what syntax is used to write it?

115: What are increment and decrement operators? What is the syntax of using them?

116: What is the value of a and b after the code execution and why?

117: What is lifetime of a variable?

118: What is the output of the following code? Explain.

119: What does 'sizeof' function return?

120: How does the meaning of increment or decrement operators change when used as prefix or postfix?

121: What arithmetic operators are present in C++?

122: Classify the different data types present in C.

123: What is a relational operator? What different types of relational operators are present in C?

124: What is a logical operator? What logical operators are available in C?

125: How are logical and (&&) and logical or (| |) operators are executed in an expression?

126: What is sign qualifier? What is the syntax of declaring it for an integer?

127: What is a size qualifier? How an integer can be declared of such type?

128: What is bit-wise operator? List the available bit-wise operators in C++?

129: How does a bitwise complement operator work?

130: How does a bitwise shift operators work?

131: What is a variable in C?

132: What rules do programmers need to follow while naming a variable in C?

133: Why are variables declared?

134: How is a variable declared so that its value can't be altered in the program once an initial value is assigned?

135: What is operator precedence?

136: What is operator associativity while evaluating an expression?

137: What is type conversion?

138: What is implicit type conversion? Use an example to explain it.

139: What are the different ways implicit type conversion can be done?

140: What is explicit type conversion?

141: How does separation by comma operator affect the evaluation of expressions?

142: What will the output be of the following program and explain why? (Integer size is 2 bytes.)

143: Explain the output of the following program. (The integer is of size 2 bytes)

144: What is will be the value of a and b in the function 'func_static' after the for loop in main function is executed till its looping condition is specified? Explain why.

145: What operators cannot be overloaded?

Macros, typedef, enum

146: What are the advantages of using a typedef?

147: What is the difference between a typedef and macro?

148: What is an enumerated data type and where can it be used?

149: What is typedef and write its syntax?

150: What is a macro in C and how is it defined?

151: What is the advantage of having macro function in a program and how is it defined?

Library Functions

152: What is the difference between exit() and abort() functions in C?

153: How do you execute a system command from a C program?

154: What are the prototypes of printf() and scanf() in C and what do printf and scanf return?

155: Explain the output of the following. (The input given by the end user is, "Are you ready.")

156: What is the difference between getch() and getche() if both can read a character?

157: How scanf() and gets() differ from each other in reading strings from an end user in C?

158: What is the output of following code and why?

Arrays

159: Explain array traversing using pointers.

160: Write a program to create and delete an array dynamically.

161: What is the difference between a string and a character array?

162: In C, what happens if a programmer is trying to access an array item in the index which exceeds the maximum size assigned to the array in its declaration?

163: Describe how an array variable name works in C.

164: Besides using the conventional method (array subscript), is there another way to access array elements?

165: Why are two dimensional arrays used?

166: How does a programmer declare and initialize two dimensional arrays?

167: How is a 1D array passed to a function in C/C++?

168: Explain the output of the following program.

169: Explain the output of the following program.

170: Explain the output of the following program.

171: Explain the output of the following program.

172: Explain the output of the following program.

173: Explain the output of the following program.

174: Explain the output of the following program.

Files in C and File Handling

175: Write a program in C to create a text file, write some text in it and then read from it.

176: What is a buffer?

177: What is a file in C?

178: What functions are involved to access the content of a file randomly?

179: Explain how to open a file in C for reading or writing operations.

180: What is the syntax of opening and closing a file in C?

181: What are file modes available that can be passed to the library function fopen() while opening a file in C?

182: What is the difference between file modes 'r+' and 'w+' while passing them as parameters to library function fopen() for opening a file?

183: How is a file opened in C++ for different operations?

Exception Handling in C++

184: What is a catch-all handler?

185: What is an exception specifier?

186: Can we use exceptions in destructors?

187: Why is exception handling required in a C program?

188: What is exception handling in C++?

189: What types of exceptions can occur during a program execution?

190: Explain asynchronous exception with an example.

191: Explain synchronous exception with an example.

192: What are the main keywords used for handling exceptions in C++?

193: What is the use of the try block in exception handling in C++?

194: What is the use of 'catch' block in exception handling in C++?

195: What is the use of 'throw' keywords for exception handling in C++?

196: What are the sequential steps that must happen to take care of exceptions in a program?

197: How can a function be controlled so that it can throw only a certain set of exceptions?

198: How can a function be declared so that it can't throw any exceptions out of its body?

199: What happens if a function raises an exception which is not mentioned in the 'exception specification list'?

200: How can the catch block be created to accept all types of exceptions (instead of just the exception types explicitly mentioned in the catch declaration).

201: What are the library functions available for handling exceptions which are not caught by the catch block?

202: What is the difference between the two library functions 'terminate' and 'unexpected'?

203: The library function terminate() eventually calls which function in the exception handling mechanism? Plus, how can a user defined function be called instead of terminate if there is no matching handler found for an exception thrown from a try block?

204: What is Stack unwinding?

Memory Areas

205: What are the operators new and delete for?

206: What does a destructor do to the memory?

207: Explain the output of the following program.

208: What is the use of the stack in C program?

209: What is the use of heap in C program?

210: Explain the output of the following program.

Classes and its Properties

211: What is an anonymous variable?

while declaring a class?

238: What is 'this' pointer?

239: What are nameless objects?

240: What is constructor overloading in C++?

241: What are default and parameterized constructors?

242: What are the limitations of static member functions of a class?

243: What are empty classes?

244: What is encapsulation?

245: How is the data hiding mechanism achieved in C++?

246: What is a pure virtual function?

247: What are abstract and concrete classes?

248: What points should a programmer remember while creating virtual functions?

249: What are live objects in C++?

250: How are virtual functions defined and why are they used?

HR Questions

1: Where do you find ideas?

2: How do you achieve creativity in the workplace?

3: How do you push others to create ideas?

4: Describe your creativity.

5: How would you handle a negative coworker?

6: What would you do if you witnessed a coworker surfing the web, reading a book, etc, wasting company time?

7: How do you handle competition among yourself and other employees?

8: When is it okay to socialize with coworkers?

9: Tell me about a time when a major change was made at your last job, and how you handled it.

10: When delegating tasks, how do you choose which tasks go to which team members?

11: Tell me about a time when you had to stand up for something you believed strongly about to coworkers or a supervisor.

12: Tell me about a time when you helped someone finish their work, even though it wasn't "your job."

13: What are the challenges of working on a team? How do you handle this?

14: Do you value diversity in the workplace?

15: How would you handle a situation in which a coworker was not accepting of someone else's diversity?

16: Are you rewarded more from working on a team, or accomplishing a task on your own?

17: Tell me about a time when you didn't meet a deadline.

18: How do you eliminate distractions while working?

19: Tell me about a time when you worked in a position with a weekly or monthly quota to meet. How often were you successful?

20: Tell me about a time when you met a tough deadline, and how you were able to complete it.

21: How do you stay organized when you have multiple projects on your plate?

22: How much time during your work day do you spend on "auto-pilot?"

23: How do you handle deadlines?

24: Tell me about your personal problem-solving process.

25: What sort of things at work can make you stressed?

26: What do you look like when you are stressed about something? How do you solve it?

27: Can you multi-task?

28: How many hours per week do you work?

29: How many times per day do you check your email?

30: How do you make decisions?

31: What are the most difficult decisions for you to make?

32: When making a tough decision, how do you gather information?

33: Tell me about a decision you made that did not turn out well.

34: Are you able to make decisions quickly?

35: What is the best way for a company to advertise?

36: Is it better to gain a new customer or to keep an old one?

37: What is the best way to win clients from competitors?

38: How do you feel about companies monitoring internet usage?

39: What is your first impression of our company?

40: Tell me about your personal philosophy on business.

41: What's most important in a business model: sales, customer service, marketing, management, etc.?

42: How do you keep up with news and emerging trends in the field?

43: Would you have a problem adhering to company policies on social media?

44: Tell me about one of the greatest problems facing X industry today.

45: What do you think it takes to be successful in our company?

46: What is your favorite part of working in this career field?

47: What do you see happening to your career in the next 10 years?

Some of the following titles might also be handy:

1. .NET Interview Questions You'll Most Likely Be Asked
2. 200 Interview Questions You'll Most Likely Be Asked
3. Access VBA Programming Interview Questions You'll Most Likely Be Asked
4. Adobe ColdFusion Interview Questions You'll Most Likely Be Asked
5. Advanced Excel Interview Questions You'll Most Likely Be Asked
6. Advanced JAVA Interview Questions You'll Most Likely Be Asked
7. Advanced SAS Interview Questions You'll Most Likely Be Asked
8. AJAX Interview Questions You'll Most Likely Be Asked
9. Algorithms Interview Questions You'll Most Likely Be Asked
10. Android Development Interview Questions You'll Most Likely Be Asked
11. Ant & Maven Interview Questions You'll Most Likely Be Asked
12. Apache Web Server Interview Questions You'll Most Likely Be Asked
13. Artificial Intelligence Interview Questions You'll Most Likely Be Asked
14. ASP.NET Interview Questions You'll Most Likely Be Asked
15. Automated Software Testing Interview Questions You'll Most Likely Be Asked
16. Base SAS Interview Questions You'll Most Likely Be Asked
17. BEA WebLogic Server Interview Questions You'll Most Likely Be Asked
18. C & C++ Interview Questions You'll Most Likely Be Asked
19. C# Interview Questions You'll Most Likely Be Asked
20. C++ Internals Interview Questions You'll Most Likely Be Asked
21. CCNA Interview Questions You'll Most Likely Be Asked
22. Cloud Computing Interview Questions You'll Most Likely Be Asked
23. Computer Architecture Interview Questions You'll Most Likely Be Asked
24. Computer Networks Interview Questions You'll Most Likely Be Asked
25. Core JAVA Interview Questions You'll Most Likely Be Asked
26. Data Structures & Algorithms Interview Questions You'll Most Likely Be Asked
27. Data WareHousing Interview Questions You'll Most Likely Be Asked
28. EJB 3.0 Interview Questions You'll Most Likely Be Asked
29. Entity Framework Interview Questions You'll Most Likely Be Asked
30. Fedora & RHEL Interview Questions You'll Most Likely Be Asked
31. GNU Development Interview Questions You'll Most Likely Be Asked
32. Hibernate, Spring & Struts Interview Questions You'll Most Likely Be Asked
33. HTML, XHTML and CSS Interview Questions You'll Most Likely Be Asked
34. HTML5 Interview Questions You'll Most Likely Be Asked
35. IBM WebSphere Application Server Interview Questions You'll Most Likely Be Asked
36. iOS SDK Interview Questions You'll Most Likely Be Asked
37. Java / J2EE Design Patterns Interview Questions You'll Most Likely Be Asked
38. Java / J2EE Interview Questions You'll Most Likely Be Asked
39. Java Messaging Service Interview Questions You'll Most Likely Be Asked
40. JavaScript Interview Questions You'll Most Likely Be Asked
41. JavaServer Faces Interview Questions You'll Most Likely Be Asked
42. JDBC Interview Questions You'll Most Likely Be Asked
43. jQuery Interview Questions You'll Most Likely Be Asked
44. JSP-Servlet Interview Questions You'll Most Likely Be Asked
45. JUnit Interview Questions You'll Most Likely Be Asked
46. Linux Commands Interview Questions You'll Most Likely Be Asked
47. Linux Interview Questions You'll Most Likely Be Asked
48. Linux System Administrator Interview Questions You'll Most Likely Be Asked
49. Mac OS X Lion Interview Questions You'll Most Likely Be Asked
50. Mac OS X Snow Leopard Interview Questions You'll Most Likely Be Asked

51. Microsoft Access Interview Questions You'll Most Likely Be Asked
52. Microsoft Excel Interview Questions You'll Most Likely Be Asked
53. Microsoft Powerpoint Interview Questions You'll Most Likely Be Asked
54. Microsoft Word Interview Questions You'll Most Likely Be Asked
55. MySQL Interview Questions You'll Most Likely Be Asked
56. NetSuite Interview Questions You'll Most Likely Be Asked
57. Networking Interview Questions You'll Most Likely Be Asked
58. OOPS Interview Questions You'll Most Likely Be Asked
59. Operating Systems Interview Questions You'll Most Likely Be Asked
60. Oracle DBA Interview Questions You'll Most Likely Be Asked
61. Oracle E-Business Suite Interview Questions You'll Most Likely Be Asked
62. ORACLE PL/SQL Interview Questions You'll Most Likely Be Asked
63. Perl Programming Interview Questions You'll Most Likely Be Asked
64. PHP Interview Questions You'll Most Likely Be Asked
65. PMP Interview Questions You'll Most Likely Be Asked
66. Python Interview Questions You'll Most Likely Be Asked
67. RESTful JAVA Web Services Interview Questions You'll Most Likely Be Asked
68. Ruby Interview Questions You'll Most Likely Be Asked
69. Ruby on Rails Interview Questions You'll Most Likely Be Asked
70. SAP ABAP Interview Questions You'll Most Likely Be Asked
71. SAP HANA Interview Questions You'll Most Likely Be Asked
72. SAS Programming Guidelines Interview Questions You'll Most Likely Be Asked
73. Selenium Testing Tools Interview Questions You'll Most Likely Be Asked
74. Silverlight Interview Questions You'll Most Likely Be Asked
75. Software Repositories Interview Questions You'll Most Likely Be Asked
76. Software Testing Interview Questions You'll Most Likely Be Asked
77. SQL Server Interview Questions You'll Most Likely Be Asked
78. Tomcat Interview Questions You'll Most Likely Be Asked
79. UML Interview Questions You'll Most Likely Be Asked
80. Unix Interview Questions You'll Most Likely Be Asked
81. UNIX Shell Programming Interview Questions You'll Most Likely Be Asked
82. VB.NET Interview Questions You'll Most Likely Be Asked
83. Windows Server 2008 R2 Interview Questions You'll Most Likely Be Asked
84. XLXP, XSLT, XPATH, XFORMS & XQuery Interview Questions You'll Most Likely Be Asked
85. XML Interview Questions You'll Most Likely Be Asked

For complete list visit

www.vibrantpublishers.com

CPSIA information can be obtained
at www.ICGtesting.com
Printed in the USA
LVOW13s1525130617
537963LV00010B/654/P